Our Favorite Vacation Beach

Ocean City, Maryland

Ellen Knop Marshall

Copyright © 2022 by Ellen Knop Marshall

All rights reserved.

ISBN 978-1-62806-348-6 (print | paperback)
ISBN 978-1-62806-349-3 (print | hardback)
ISBN 978-1-62806-350-9 (print | ebook)

Library of Congress Control Number 2022906545

Published by Salt Water Media
29 Broad Street, Suite 104
Berlin, MD 21811
www.saltwatermedia.com

Images are courtesy of the author and/or used with permission

Our Favorite Vacation Beach

Ocean City, Maryland

Mom, Dolores Knop Sprissler,
reading on deck at a bayside condo - 2010
Photo by Eugene Marshall

Dedication

This Ocean City love letter is dedicated to two of my family members. My mother, Dolores Knop Sprissler, introduced me to this wondrous place as a toddler. My husband, Eugene Marshall, supported me throughout the research, interviews, writing and editing phases. I would never have stayed true to this project without their inspiration and confidence in me.

Thanks to...

My editors, Michele Rubin, my comprehensive editor and Rich Storrs, my copy editor, both part of The Writer's Ally. Their wisdom and experience helped to polish and craft this writing. Business and Publishing Manager, Julie Haase, successfully kept me on track. Julie knew instinctively when to apply ego balm. My publishers at Salt Water Media, Stephanie L. Fowler and Andrew Heller, you made it happen beautifully.

Contents

From a Seagull's Perspective 1

My Ocean City 5

Ocean City History 9

The Destination Beach 25

The Boardwalk 35

Where We Stay 73

Where We Eat 113

Where We Worship 133

Iconic Characters 159

Afterthoughts 177

Background Information 179

Acknowledgements 180

Endnotes 185

Ellen's Favorite Places 199

From a Seagull's Perspective

WHOOSHHH the hurricane winds are building up to a crescendo. The winds are pushing the surf further onto shore, alarming the surf fishermen making an early morning catch – or so they thought. "Looks like we're in for something big. Look at that horizon getting darker. Won't be much of a catch today," Samuel told his fishing mates. "Yep, let's pack it in," agreed. "Look, even the birds know it's a comin."

The skies turn gray, then black, and the wind begin to make a sound more like a train coming through than a 60 mph wind. The men pull up their nets, tether down their catch buckets and pull the hood of their slickers over their rain-beaten heads. Soon they were gone.

CRACKKKKK. Henrietta, the seagull looking for breakfast for her brood is holding onto her chicklings for dear life. The piece of pier she perched upon just gave way and she took off with her family seconds before it was too late. They are too young yet to fly any distance.

Henrietta and her chicks float above the wood planks turned projectiles by the winds. On the sand she spies some conch shells which seem large enough to protect her charges while the storm rages. They seem far enough away from the surf and are anchored by the sand dunes. So, she quickly pushes them with her beak and wings into the shells and majestically flies off to higher ground. "Goodbye, my lovelies. Mom will be back soon."

Crashhh. All around humans are moving to higher ground as the waves grow fiercer and fiercer. The wooden fishing shanties eject their occupants, who were thinking they had found shelter. This storm is much, much bigger than anyone – human or seagull – had seen in years.

Eventually the surf encroaches into paths never used, over banks that had stood firm for decades. The sea proves too powerful to hold in place man-made barriers. The landscape and seascape are changing as Henrietta watches from a shelter she has found. After two days of torrential rain, the barrier island could no longer hold back the surge of water. She hopes against hope that her chicks are okay.

Henrietta flies against the high winds to check on her children. There, she sees two, no three, of her chicklings peeping from their shells. Where is Dody? She swoops down and one-by-one carries her soggy children to the top floor of a structure still standing on the beach. Now to find Dody.

From the sky Henrietta hardly recognizes her Ocean City. The house where that nice family of 5 children is flattened. Hopefully, they all got to high ground. And the pier where she fed each morning was wiped out, its remains floating in the ocean. And wait, what is this? The inlet seems completely changed; the south side of town is a ghost-like mirage eerily peeping out from the deluge.

Everything that was familiar to her from the sky has vanished. Mother Nature showed Henrietta that she was the master builder and destroyer. None of the usual perches for her family withstood the wind and rain. Family, got to get back to the young ones. They need their Momma – all of them, but especially Dody.

Kerplop, kerplop, kerplop the pounding raindrops almost obscure her vision. After what seems to be hours of searching for Dody, the evening brings calm. The rain stops. There is something so peaceful about Ocean City after a storm. All seems as if her world is right again. Except for ...

She lights upon the broken and shattered remains of the shelters that once stood near the pier. Where is the pier? Where is the divide between the ocean and the bay? Where is her little one? Panic takes over again. Could this new tide take away more than what men made?

Henrietta searches along the beach and spots a conch shell wriggling. Ahhhh. Dody is inside, shivering with fear, but happy to see her mom. Henrietta nestles her beak into Dody's neck and prunes her feathers, entangled with debris. All is right with her world again.

Henrietta will later chirp to her grands about the Storm of 1933 which almost took her family.

So much has happened in Ocean City since the Great Storm of 1933. The tremendous power of the surf was a turning point for what was once a lazy fishing town. The inlet was formed from the hand of Mother Nature and this Atlantic Paradise was forever changed.

In the following pages we can together relive many of our best Ocean City memories. The sights, the sounds, the smells and the tastes of this family resort create such pleasant experiences that we come back, again and again. Hold on for a wonderful ride!

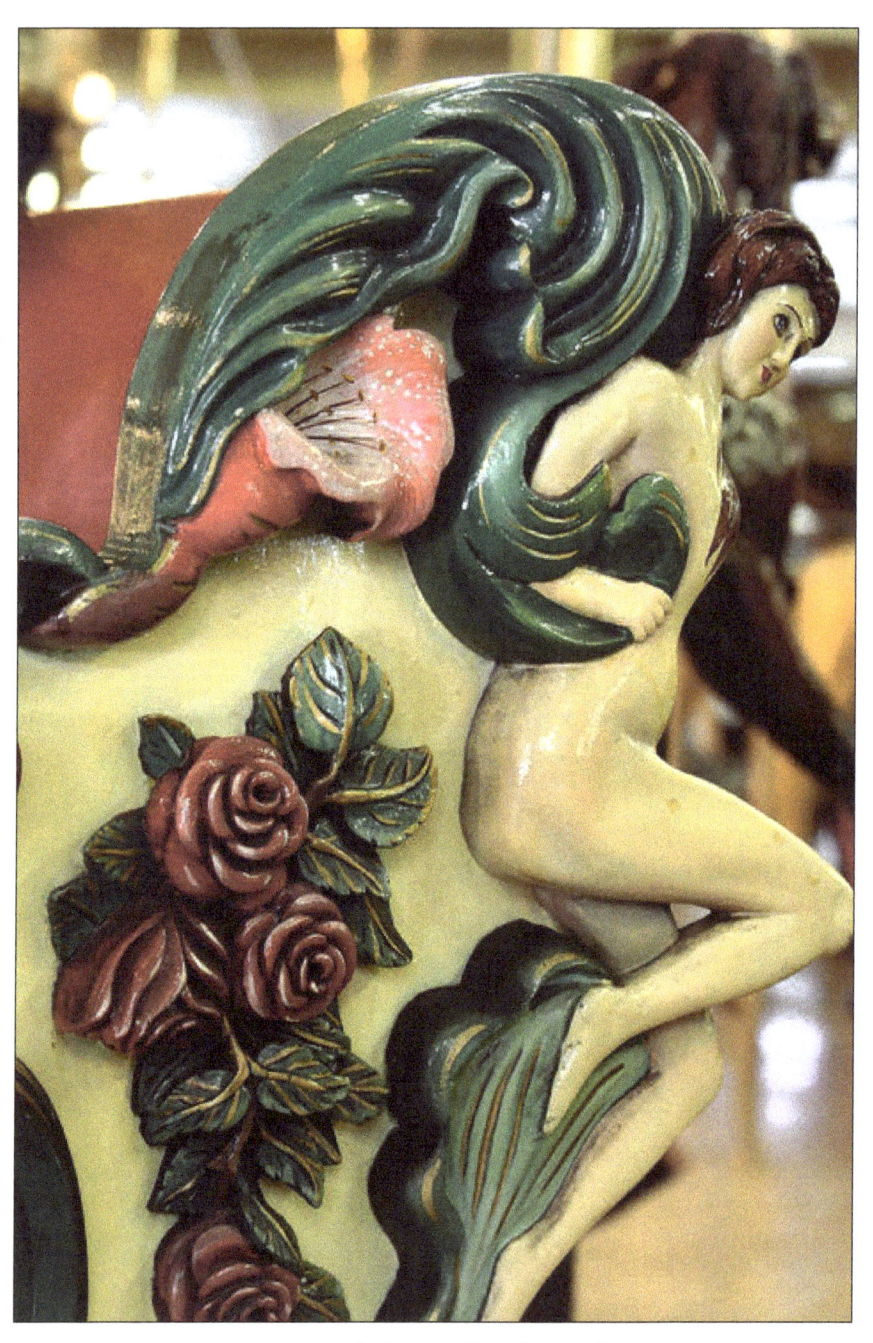

Trimper's Carousel Back Panel
Photo by Ellen Marshall

My Ocean City

A May October

Some years May slides in as
A hot streak in Oriole orange
Or a white and pink peak of honeysuckle
Climbing through the neighbor's fence

Or it shades itself through the
Fingers of mulberry perches
Where red red cardinals
Await a love

It's never too late
For spring
For tending passions
Like the rhythm of
Words
Kerplunking

Ellen Marshall

I love you, Ocean City Maryland. Your scents cling to my skin from the moment I cross the Route 50 Bridge. You send the salt water straight to my nostrils to greet me. Your unique brine is your welcome mat. I follow that aroma straight to my Atlantic and respond, "Hello, Ocean City. I'm back."

Even the sand has its own signature scent of crushed seashells and sunscreen. That is what fills my nose from an open window of our rented apartment and beckons me to stake out my place for the day at 7:30 am.

You know to send those wafts of Thrasher's French fries when I step onto the boardwalk. Doughroller Pizza smells find me and invite me to plan a meal at Third. I wonder where that lovely smell of grilled onions is coming from? Is it the Bull on the Beach pit beef sandwich at Second Street or Boog Powell's foot long at the pier? The lovely aroma of crabs steamed in Old Bay drift onto my path every block along the walk.

I love you, Ocean City Maryland. Your sights tell me that I am home again. The brightly colored water tower near the Sinepuxent Bay spells out your signature. I turn to the right to see the lovely new West Ocean City homes almost touching the water. The Angler Restaurant sign beckons next. At Division and Baltimore your White Marlin sculpture, generously spouting a stream of water, reminds me of the industry that birthed you. As I turn onto Baltimore Avenue, brightly painted clapboard houses and hotels beckon me to register there. Small gift shops and the slap dash Ocean Gallery façade remind me that you are my one and only, Ocean City.

I love you, Ocean City Maryland. Your sounds announce that I am no longer in Baltimore. The rhythmic pounding of the surf is your calling card, my alarm in the morning, my relaxing background mid-day and my lullaby at night. The calls of other beach-goers to one another, "Where are we going to eat tonight, hon," finds its way to my hotel balcony. Music from a nearby radio is no intrusion when I sit upon my beach chair. I recognize the sounds of the Beach Boys proclaiming, "Surf City, here I come..." or The Drifters crooning "Under the Boardwalk you can fall in love..." as well as a Bach Sonata or a Pink release. As I share my beach space with others, we often drift into casual conversations. From near the Ocean City Pier, I hear the oompah-pah of Trimper's carousel or the Haunted House's eerie creature laugh. I delight at the sound of laughing children as they run into the surf. When I am away from the Ocean, I only have to place a conch shell against my ear and your surf sounds return. All is well with the world when I am with you, Ocean City.

I have loved you, Ocean City Maryland most of my life. From the time I was a toddler my parents drove us the 150 miles for our week down the ocean. I hold in my heart a lovely memory of my Dad walking me and my 10 year old brother, Carl, out upon a sand bar at 1st street. Dad cries, "Look, kids," and picks up a conch shell. "Listen," he promises," you can hear the ocean inside." I display that shell near my computer desk today.

We continued that trek with our three children, sometimes with my Mom and siblings and their families during the same week. We would stay for years at King's Cottages, operated by Miss Carrie and her husband in early August. Later we frequented the Lambos Apartments, greeted by Gus Lambros who would notice how much our kids had grown over the winter. I taught our kids to jump the waves, just as my parents had. As they got older, I delighted in the secrets we shared in that space where the sky meets the Atlantic.

Night at Ocean City is magical. The whack-a-mole operator shouts as we walk past, "Come on, kids, try your luck here." The rat a tat tat of the shooting gallery tempts us to see if we can knock the frog off his lily pad perch. Some evenings it would take a few tries to get my girls or son to follow me onto the Riptide for a heart-dropping journey through the loop de loop upside down ride at 60 mph. "Yeah, can we do it again, Mom?"

Today we love to take our young grandkids to our favorite hotels like The Paradise Plaza at 9th and the Boardwalk and the nearby Lankford, one of the remaining family-owned hotels with a large porch fronting the boardwalk. We build sandcastles, loll on beach chairs and watch for a passing dolphin school. At night Granddad takes them to the 9th Street Arcade to win tickets playing skee ball, as he did with their mother.

Ahh. I trust the kids will someday return with their children, walk out onto the beach at their arrival and say "We're back, Ocean City." I believe this because happy memories are the stuff of which Ocean City is made.

Ocean City History

"All the world's a stage, and all the men and women merely players: they have their exits and their entrances: and one man in his time plays many parts, his acts being seven ages."

William Shakespeare

As You Like It, Act II Scene VII Line 139

Welcome to Ocean City
Photo by Eugene Marshall

It is remarkable that the 10 mile area of land along the Atlantic Ocean coast in Maryland had such humble beginnings. I see a thriving beach community, full of life and entertainment. From the beautiful sandy beach to the glorious swimming to the celebrated nightlife Ocean City, Maryland is an international attraction.

This paradise where I have spent countless weeks all during my life took more than three centuries to evolve. Residents and entrepreneurs shared a vision that sparked this metamorphosis. Ocean City is so much more than its geography.

Pre 1600 - 1931

The Ocean City before the 20th century had a very modest, even unappealing, landscape. Its major draw for the Native Americans who settled there before immigrants from England was the bounty of the sea. Oysters, clams, mussels and fish were abundant. In a recent Maryland Public Television documentary "Eatin' Oysters" these early settlers are eating the world-renowned Chesapeake oyster and piling their shells onto a midden.[1]

Native Americans "lived in permanent houses made of wood and bark," according to Michael Morgan.[2]

The barrier island which became Ocean City, Maryland was home to the ..."Pocomoke, Chincoteague, and Assateague Indians of the Nanticoke tribe..."[3] These first nations probably fished and hunted for centuries before white men signed a treaty with the Nanticoke peoples on October 3, 1704 .

Geographers describe Ocean City as part of a barrier spit. The land area goes north along the Atlantic Ocean to South

Bethany, Delaware, and Fenwick Island, Delaware. It has a total area of 36.37 square miles. Its southern border is separated from Assateague Island by the inlet created by a storm in 1933.

For the next six decades English settlers to the Eastern Shore of Maryland used separate treaties with the first nations to lay claim to this prosperous land beside the sea. Native-American chiefs of the Six Nations on June 30, 1744 gave up all claims to land in this new Maryland colony. This treaty allowed the Maryland General Assembly to purchase all land claims in Maryland. When the Nanticoke relinquished their land claims and received compensation on June 18, 1768, some native peoples moved to other colonies in what is now

Assateague Sculpture at Inlet
Photo by Eugene Marshall

the Carolinas, Virginia, Delaware, Pennsylvania, Illinois and Ohio. Several of the Nanticoke families purchased land and moved to Princess Anne and Salisbury, Maryland.

When you drive along US Route 50, a major thoroughfare which runs from California to Ocean City, or from I-95, you will see names reflecting this rich heritage: Assateaque, Potomac, Rappahanock, Chickahominy, Wicomico, Delaware, and Occoquan, and Pocomoke. A statue of an Assateague of the Nanticoke Nation by Peter Wolf Toth at the Ocean City inlet stands as a tribute to our first peoples. It is one of Toth's series "Trail of the Whispering Giants" in all 50 states.

Meanwhile English settlers in 1660 were moving to the Eastern Shore of Maryland. Many of them were convicts, indentured servants and slaves of color. Lord Baltimore held title to most of Maryland, including Worcester County, but then lost the land. These early settlers used the island mainly for grazing livestock.

The land which became the Eastern Shore was given to the Calvert family in 1632 as part of a British land grant.

After Charles I signed the 1632 charter granting Maryland to the Calverts, the Virginia colonists maneuvered so the new colony would fail. Charles I's colonial governor in Virginia, John Harvey, wrote back to London that the Virginians *"would rather knock their cattell on the heads then sell them to Maryland."*[4]

Lord Calvert lost the property rights to Maryland for a time. In February 1715 England restored the land to Benedict Leonard Calvert, 4th Lord Baltimore. Englishman Thomas Fenwick owned the land which became Ocean City.

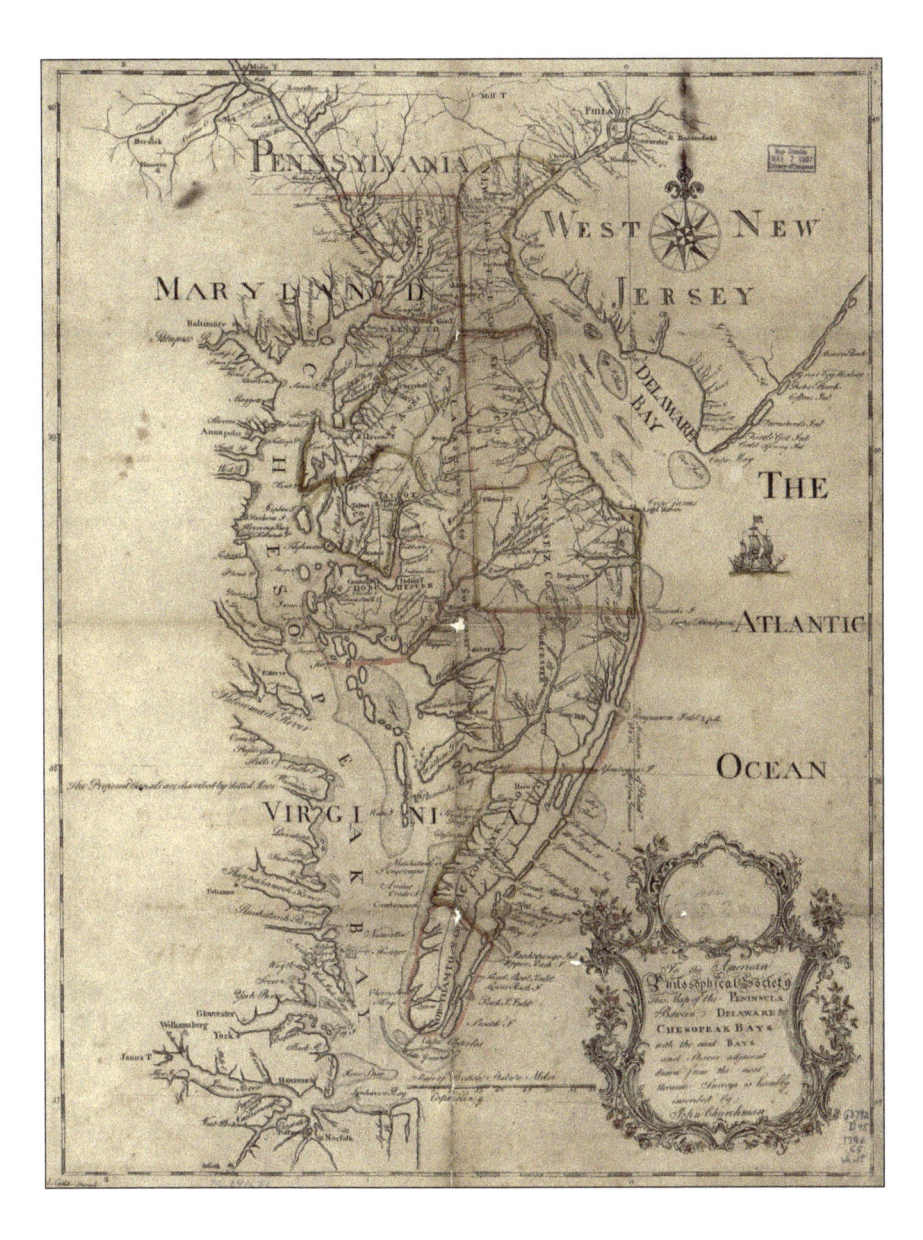

Map of the Delmarva Peninsula circa 1786
Public domain image courtesy of the Library of Congress,
Prints and Photographs Division

Map from the Maryland State Archives Website, Reprinted from https://www.msa.maryland.gov (Annapolis, MD 2022)

1874 to 1932

The earliest visitors to Ocean City, Maryland routinely traveled from Baltimore and Philadelphia by rail. When they arrived, they could stay at one of the few large hotels. The Atlantic (1875), the Plimhimmon (1874) and the Belmont

(1905). A beach cottage owned by Gertrude Purnell Parker, Josephine Massey and Susan Dickerson Mason also housed travelers. The Baltimore, Chesapeake and Atlantic Railway train brought riders to the station. There they were met by young men with carts who carried the luggage to their rented lodging places for the week or month.

Cars made the trip by another route. The barrier island of Ocean City is in the easternmost county of Maryland and is separated from the most populous areas of Maryland and Pennsylvania by the Chesapeake Bay. Travelling there before the automobile was an eight to ten hour adventure. Few people owned cars pre- WWI. Taking a train or boat to Berlin, then a ferry over the Sinepuxent Bay to the island, was the usual method of travel. In 1952 the first bridge over the bay was erected. That structure gave carriage or train traffic more direct access via Baltimore Avenue. The first train station was located on the east side of Baltimore Avenue between Somerset and Wicomico Streets. The first auto ride was driven by owner Everett E. Jackson with passengers Allen F. Benjamin and J. Edgar Igams. They travelled along the railroad trestle crossing the Bay.

Trains brought early Ocean City visitors onto the island by way of a bridge across the Sinepuxent Bay. At the time it was the quickest mode of travel. For example, automobiles and buses leaving Baltimore had to travel north through Delaware or southwest around the Chesapeake Bay's counties to reach the island. Michael Morgan tells us about the farm roads of Worcester County that were covered "with a layer of crushed stone to give bicyclists a better surface on which to ride."

"Original railroad terminal at Baltimore Avenue and S. Division Street."
Reproduced by permission of Ocean City Life Savings Museum
https://www.oceancitymd/oc-history

The McDaniel

The McDaniel was part of the Baltimore, Chesapeake & Atlantic Railroad. The line to Ocean City started at McDaniel on the Chesapeake Bay with stops at St. Michaels, Royal, Easton, Tanyard, Bethlehem, Preston, Elwood, Hurlock, Rhodesdale, Reids Grove, Vienna, Mardela Springs, Hebron, Salisbury, Walstons, Parsonsburg, Pittsville, Willards, Whaleyville, Saint Martin, Berlin, Diricksons, Sinepuxent, and West Ocean City.

The McDaniel came into Ocean City by way of a bridge. Alan Snyder tells us:

The old line was also called the Ocean City Railroad.

> The tracks went to the docks on the intercoastal waterway. In 1978, the tracks were still there and had trees as big as 1 foot growing in the center. The ROW is hard to find — the forest has taken it back. But the tracks are there if you look off US-50.

And on a personal note:

> Back in the 1960s during my teen years, I used to closely observe the segments of this line, along with other DelMarVa branches, still in operation while traveling to Ocean City for summer vacationing with my aunt and uncle. Riding east along US 50 after crossing the Bay Bridge, I picked up where the old Love Point-Rehoboth Beach B&E line paralleled the highway. Where it crossed creeks, the wooden bridge supports were still intact. At Kent Narrows bridge a couple old trestle bents still existed, and east of the bridge I could see a path of very rotted crossties here and there up to the US50/US301 split. The rails ended about half mile east of that point in Queenstown, which still had rail service into the early 1970s.[5]

Sheri Reno talks about the typical journey by boat and rail:

> The trip would begin by leaving Baltimore by one of the steamboats which would wind through the waterways until reaching the railroad yards of the Wicomico and Pocomoke Railroad in Salisbury. From Salisbury, the visitors would ride one of the wood-burning trains to the shores of the Sinepuxent Bay in West Ocean City.

The all-day journey would finally end after the visitors crossed the bay by ferry or small boats to Ocean City. In 1876, a wooden railroad bridge was built over the Sinepuxent Bay. The bridge entered the town at South Division Street and ran up to a depot on Baltimore Avenue. When trains were not using the bridge, planks were placed in between the ties which allowed walkers, horses and buggies to cross the bridge.[6]

By the time automobiles made the trek to the barrier island on July 1, 1904 beachgoers found their destination in less time. That provided the weekender or day tripper with much more time to spend at the sea or on the boardwalk. The Ocean City boardwalk distinguishes this resort from most other beaches which border the Atlantic Ocean.

Branding the Boardwalk

The use of a walkway made of boards is not unique to Ocean City. Seaside resorts in England used boardwalks for strolling between hotels, restaurants and entertainment venues. Soon that custom crossed the Atlantic and has become one of the amenities that make Ocean City so picturesque.

The boardwalk structure has morphed from its beginnings. At first the Atlantic Hotel and seaside cottages wanted to assist beachgoers to walk between lodging and eating places. Then, they simply laid down boards along the sand and took them in at night.

Eventually the boardwalk became a more permanent structure and expanded to its present 1.7 miles. In the picture above from the 1920s one can see about 18 inches to 2

The Mount Pleasant Hotel showing the height of the boardwalk

feet from the top of the sand. Because natural wood takes a beating from the salt water and sand that drifts onto it as the wind blows, planks have to be routinely replaced. The town rebuilt a new boardwalk that hugged the beach closer, and that formula continues to this day.

The Ocean City Council voted to replace the existing boards in 2013. The council polled residents and businesspersons to ask if they wanted to pay the high cost of pure wood replacement, go to a concrete walkway, or try a mixture of wood and a manmade material that would be less expensive than all wood. The poll results came in that the mixed wood structure could continue the look of the boardwalk everyone loved, yet cut down on the replacement costs.

DJ Batman, one of the most popular entertainers appearing regularly at Club Seacrets, calls the Ocean City boardwalk "The greatest sidewalk in America." From its beginnings the

*Boardwalk reconstruction is shown below 8th Street.
Photo by Ellen Marshall*

boardwalk provided beach goers with a wooden walkway to the beach, the restaurants, the gift shops, the pier and the entertainment venues. It is a symbolic yardstick for anything Ocean: distance is often measured by how far a building is from the Boardwalk. "You'll find the Ocean Gallery about four streets down, just where the boardwalk turns," a local directs a visitor to his destination.

Through the years the Ocean City boardwalk has remained an iconic image for this Atlantic Paradise. Just as Chicago's or San Francisco's or Baltimore's roads link us to the Wrigley Building, the Embarcadero and Camden Yards, the Ocean City Boardwalk transports us to sights, sounds and experiences the summer promises. This boardwalk, like the pier and early wooden structures lining the Ocean took a severe hit during the Storm of 1933.

1933 to present day
"The Mother Storm of Them All"

The storm which came into Ocean City, Maryland on August 22, 1933 forever changed the resort and its residents. The city's website condenses that story:

> The Ocean City Inlet was formed during a major hurricane in August 1933, which also destroyed the train tracks across the Sinepuxent Bay. The inlet separated what is now Ocean City from Assateague Island. The Army Corps of Engineers took advantage of nature's intervention and made the inlet at the south end of Ocean City permanent. The inlet eventually helped to establish Ocean City as an important Mid-Atlantic fishing port as it offered easy

Inlet created by the storm of 1933. Reproduced by permission from Ocean City Life Savings Museum. https://www.oceancitymd/oc-history (Maryland: Ocean City Life Savings Museum, 2022)

access to the fishing grounds of the Atlantic Ocean.[7]

Besides fishing, residents and investors saw opportunities to grow and market Ocean City as a place to relax in the sun, to get away from the pace of city living. The early modest cottages and family homes were either expanded or torn down to make way for places for vacationers to rent. The boardwalk was rebuilt to accommodate new eateries and entertainment venues.

The disaster of 1933 transformed the fledgling resort into a destination. Sun lovers from mainly Baltimore, Washington, DC and Wilmington saw Ocean City as a relatively quick journey to paradise. And they came and they came.

Entertainment had always been a focus since the early resort days, but it took on extra importance after 1933. The Pier Building at the entrance to the city pier was built in 1926 for dancing, skating rink, bowling, playing pool and eating. The building façade still exists as an entryway to the rides at the pier. The inlet appropriately showcases the early history with a Native American sculpture. Harrison's Harborwatch Inn, the Frog Bar as well as unique shops and the Ocean City Life Saving Museum bring many thousands of visitors to the inlet each year.

The storm of 1933, the booming automobile industry and the building of the Chesapeake Bay Bridge in 1952 drew many more people to the Eastern Shore and Ocean City, Maryland. Investors from the surrounding large cities built clapboard hotels and rooming houses to accommodate overnighters eager to enjoy these seaside pleasures.

The city expanded its limits gradually to the Delaware State line and westward along the Sinepuxent Bay. Big mon-

Ocean City Life Saving Museum at Inlet.
Photo by Eugene Marshall

ey built the communities of Montego Bay, Isle of Wight and Ocean Pines on the bayside and Glen Riddle off Route 50. The 1970's expanded Ocean City by building more than 10,000 high rise condominium units with an ocean view. That trend continues through the present day, inviting a year-round swell of the visitors every season of the year.

The sleepy fishing village of 19th century Ocean City became what we love today, an Atlantic Paradise of fun and sun. The beach community has created the unique blend of relaxation by day and the excitement of entertainment opportunities by night. It is these pioneers and entrepreneurs who had a vision and put in the blood, sweat and tears to make their visions reality.

The Old Boardwalk
Photo courtesy of Catherine Monius Merkel

The Destination Beach

"To wake at dawn with a winged heart and give thanks for another day of loving."

Kahlil Gibran

It was the summer of 1954 when I discovered that magical creatures lived in the Ocean City, Maryland waters. My father, a Baltimore City firefighter, walked my older brother and me out on a sand bar during low tide. All of a sudden Dad's face lit up with a smile. He reached down, pulled up a conch shell and held it to my ears. I heard the same sound of the waves lapping around my little feet inside that shell. I thought this was a miracle and that my Dad was a magician. So it was then that my love affair with Ocean City began.

Those of us living on the East Coast have many beaches to choose from. The mid-Atlantic abuts the Atlantic Ocean and dozens of rivers and bays. Where we go to sun is as much dictated by our eagerness to recapture all of the memorable moments of our youth as it is by our desires to share those joys with our children and grandchildren. What I try to recount in this book, although seeming deeply personal to me, is a shared galaxy of experiences that echo in the space of many of our hearts over the past century.

These shared experiences and memories of Ocean City, Maryland form the cultural fabric of this mid-Atlantic vacation destination. Certainly, the grit and determination of the first year round settlers is a foundation of that culture. Add to that quality the foresight of the working classes from the lower Eastern Shore of Maryland. They could envision a playground for future beach goers and were willing to commute to build this paradise. Finally what made the town a reality was the hope of the 105 investors of the Atlantic Hotel Corporation who in 1875 paid out the $25 per plot investment.

For over 140 years millions of people have been attracted to this nine + mile stretch of land bordered by the Atlantic Ocean to the east, the Sinepuxent Bay to the west, the Delaware state line to the north and Assateague Island to the south. Their experiences and Ocean City's growth run parallel with our fascination with how different a beach is to other living areas. At the beach one's mind turns away from work and daily stressors. Beach-goers lose their normal garb and attempt to live in swimsuits and sandals for at least half the day. They think creative thoughts, they write poetry, they scream on the Tidal Wave rollercoaster, they read dime store novels, they eat different food, and they just ... sit in a beach chair and watch the tides.

The resort dear to the half-million of us who vacation there every year and the 7,000[8] who are permanent residents took nearly 85 years to become the thriving beach town it is today. This chapter will highlight some of the major events that changed the barrier island into a premier summer destination on the mid-Atlantic coast.

Like most of the United States, the land was initially home to Native Americans. The first peoples seemed to be drawn to the roaming livestock and the bounty of the sea. During colonial times English settlers saw the opportunity to turn Ocean City's natural treasure into a way of life.

George and Suzanne Hurley track the initial transition to a beach community when in 1872:

> ...a prominent group of Eastern Shore, Baltimore and Philadelphia businessmen visited the beach to select a site for development...sold four thousand shares of stock with a par value of twenty-five dollars each...surveyed and subdivided into 205 building lots...[9]

George Hurley[10] tells the condensed story of how a restful resort where city dwellers came on a train to relax and get away from city air and bustle developed into a thriving summer play land with million dollar properties. The years between 1872 and the present are overflowing with stories of fortunes made and lost and made again.

On the website of the Ocean City Life-Saving Museum people were invited to submit memories of times gone by. George Hurley describes the resort in the 1950s:

> Ocean City at that time extended from the Inlet to Fifteenth Street. To the north was Worcester County, which was pine groves, marsh meadows, and sand dunes. A narrow two lane concrete road ran to Delaware. Along it were a handful of private summer cottages nestled among the dunes, and at least one roadhouse named the "Lucky Lindy" (after the aviator Lindbergh.) Along the west side of town where today's St. Louis Avenue is, there was marsh meadow north of 1st Street. The fire department volunteers still used a Model A Ford that was

purchased in the 1930s as a front line truck. Our school was today's City Hall. The school had a small enrollment (there was a total of 30 boys, in grades nine through twelve). The Town was so small that when my class of 1952 traveled to the University of Maryland to become the first Eastern Shore team to ever win a state basketball championship, the city leaders were concerned. They were afraid that so many citizens might attend the game that there would not be enough men available in the event of a major fire in town!...

1950 was one of the first post-World War II years that saw the beginning of new construction in Ocean City. Apartment buildings were being built in the north end of town (8th Street to 15th Street.) One refrain that was discussed in barbershops, soda fountains, hardware stores, and elsewhere was that Ocean City was being over built and that the town would never see enough vacationers to rent all of the new apartments.[11]

These stories are recounted from witnesses to these events. They explain why we return to Ocean City, Maryland again and again. Perhaps their experiences sound similar to others who vacation in Nantucket or the Outer Banks of North Carolina. However, the people who built Ocean City by working the land and harvesting the rich bounty of the Sinepuxent Bay and the Mid-Atlantic were different from any other beach anywhere. George and Susan Hurley explain this difference:

> Earlier generations were geographically isolated in Worcester County; this caused the culture to develop with a leisurely pace and life-style. The land and waters of this section of the Eastern Shore of Maryland contributed greatly to the serenity...but the slow pace and ease of living created a personality most regard as very sociable, but plainspoken, with a touch of salt.[12]

Bound with this touch of salt is a gritty determination to prosper. All of the chapters in this book reflect one theme: the people of Ocean City created and continually recreate this Atlantic paradise through old fashioned hard work. Their reality continues to be: you got to work to make a buck. A visitor rarely enters a mid-sized or large Ocean City business when the CEO is not behind the front counter or walking through to check customer satisfaction.

To complete the winning formula these pioneers also needed the help of Mother Nature, the federal and state government, and the growth of transportation to catapult their vision into a successful beach town with 450,000 visitors a year.[13]

My methodology in preparing to write this, my love story to Ocean City, was to try to unearth that one characteristic of the full-time residents which describes its essence. Beyond the observations of George Hurley cited above, I saw and heard a deep connection to life centered on the Atlantic Ocean and Sinepuxent Bay. Most of their lives were involved in fishing and crabbing, preparing seafood for their families and visitors. Or they are constructing homes, hotels, retail outlets, cultural venues and restaurants to make life in Ocean

City more complete. In times of disaster this community pulls together, knit like fishing nets to one another.

The story of Ocean City is told in this book by the many of us who experience it's impossible-to-resist qualities. Our experiences will also be placed in the context of its history. One cannot truly understand this resort without a thumbnail sketch of the major forces which shaped its identity.

Time for the Beach.
Photo by Eugene Marshall

The Mighty, Mighty Ocean

Our lives are woven by stories. At times the threads of these weavings intertwine in a way that demands a "Yes, I also remember the way the sunsets cooled us after a long day of jumping in and out of the waves. But then we would..."

Many things about the 1960s in Ocean City resonate in a multi-layered fabric about freedom and new experiences among baby boomers. Maybe it is just that it was a post WWII era when coming-of-age meant wanting to forget duty and soak-in as much fun as possible. During this simpler time, I was willing to sleep on a relative's kitchen floor so that I could have a summer week "down the ocean, hon." My family's stays were all below Eighth Street where the traditional apartment houses and hotels rented at reasonable rates and we were able to get to the beach in a hundred seagull steps.

Ocean City was the place where the lucky kids worked summers. If we were only there for a week, we sat on the boardwalk at night, listening to the conversations of waitresses, t-shirt shop cashiers and lifeguards. Of course, I never realized that those "fortunate few" barely made enough to keep a roof over their heads AND eat.

It was a magical time to be at Ocean City, Maryland. I sat on a beach blanket with my siblings, watching the cute guys

Siblings and friends on the OC Beach 1969

pass by on the sand. We'd flirt with the telescope photographers and pose in a pyramid just to try to get invited to that night's party. We seldom bought the telescope print, but the picture stayed in our mind's eye. Each night we'd walk the boards out to the pier and inlet, stopping for a shaved ice or Candy Kitchen sundae or Dolles saltwater taffy, maybe a ride on the roller coaster.

Ocean City even smelled different from Baltimore. Before air-conditioned cars and buses, you could take in the wondrous aroma of the salt water as you drove over the OC bridge. The excitement of promises wafted in that scent.

Much has changed since then at Ocean City, but much remains bubbling up in my heart each time I take in that magic salt air. We're here, Ocean City, let the summer begin!

Jumping the Waves

Naturally, it is the proximity to the Atlantic Ocean that draws us to Ocean City. Like responding to a siren call, residents and visitors stream to the water's edge, some of them at daybreak. On a summer's day there is nothing like waking to the rhythmic surf pounding the shoreline and the smell of fresh salt water. We come to relax, to watch the beach crowd, to surf and to swim. And, except for a few outliers, we come with others.

Many of us learn early in life that it is great fun to wade out into the water where the waves are breaking. We watch Moms and Dads and Grandparents or older siblings show the young ones how to navigate the waves, just as most of us were taught. We see the "instructor" hold both hands of the child, sides against the surf. Then they wait for that wave to peak and watch them be lifted aloft by the might of the ocean. Parents all over the world use that technique in the Pacific and the Indian Oceans, probably even in the Mediterranean, Aegean and Red Seas. It works, especially because an older stronger person holds their charge firmly by the hands.

That first deep dip into the ocean might feel a bit chilly, but once one is mid-chest deep, the water feels so good. Jumping the waves is so relaxing: your body just floats up and down with the wave's cresting.

Jumping the waves can be mystical. I feel one with nature, indeed one with everyone else swimming in the Atlantic Ocean at that moment up and down the U.S. coastline. Sometimes I speak to their spirits, calling them to jump with me. On my first day in the water I quickly recall why I have come these 150 miles.

Ocean City took off as a summer destination after four major events: the invention of the motor car; the erection of a bridge into the island; the great storm of August 22, 1933, which formed an inlet connecting the Sinepuxent Bay with the Atlantic Ocean; and the opening of the Chesapeake Bay Bridge in 1952.

Painting on the wall panel of Trimper's Carousel
Photo by Ellen Marshall

The Boardwalk

New Year

Look for the miracles
In small spaces
They won't be in the glaring light
Or the blaring static of
Loudspeakers
They creep quietly
Behind the living places
As stealthily as the summer breath
Of robins
Alongside the swish of wings
Away
I miss them more than I
Mark them...
No more
Waiting for the coming
Of miracles
Only live
Within them.

Ellen Knop Marshall

The 2½ mile Ocean City boardwalk is magical. At one and the same moment it connects strollers wearing shorts to modern day entertainment and restaurants while it reaches back to another time. Then well-dressed ladies and gentlemen twirled to live band music from the Pier Ballroom and a couple could order a complete Delmarva chicken dinner for $2.25. Lives are interwoven across generations. Families rediscover shared glee on the Tidal Wave roller coaster and children's eyes show delight in the glitter and the neon – all on the iconic Ocean City boardwalk. There's no other place like it in the world.

From its earliest days, Ocean City has been called a family resort. Many of those vacationing families migrated from Baltimore and other Maryland and Pennsylvania towns for their week at the beach. When those families included teens, or soon-to-be teens, the young found a way to meet up with their friends. In the 1960s and '70s that place was often the Boardwalk at 9th Street.

The Boardwalk During Cruisin' Week 2019
Photo by Eugene Marshall

Like other mid-Atlantic beaches such as Dewey, Rehoboth, and the Jersey Shore, Ocean City, Maryland became a mecca for young sun lovers. In the '60s, the age of the Beachboys ("Little Surfer", "Surfin USA"), younger teens connected with their friends on the beach or the boardwalk. Older teens might have been fortunate enough to have a job for the summer at Ocean City. A blogger, Camping with Kids writes "... I go there a lot. Even met my wife there at the Sheraton Lounge. (LOL) She worked for the Trimpers as a teen-ager, and I had numerous summer jobs in OC too. It was the 'in' place to work for graduating seniors."[14] The minimum wage jobs may have barely paid the rent and a splurge on a pizza a week, but it didn't matter. They temporarily lived at the beach and knew they'd have a wonderful time at the parties and clubs.

Burt Raughley recalls his youth working in Ocean City:

> Fortunately, in the summers of '49 and '50 I worked for John Dale Showell managing one of his beach umbrella stands, along with my buddies George Hurley and Bill Brown. I walked to work at North Division Street and the Boardwalk from my home at 107 St. Louis Ave. Good money, too, $20.00 weekly gross, for seven days. The teenage social aspects of working on the beach made up for the meager salary. Plus, many evenings I would set up pins in Mr. Showell's bowling alley, and earn another couple of dollars.[15]

"Summertime, summertime, sum, sum summertime," as the lyrics to "Summertime, Summertime" by the Jamies begin. Recalling those lyrics brings many of us back to that time in our lives.

At the middle of the 20th century, Ocean City began its metamorphosis to become a thriving resort town. Today, besides the beach and water fun, much of the vacationers' activity centers around the ocean walkway called "the boardwalk." This chapter takes you to the amusements, the art, t-shirt and tchotchkes shops, the shooting gallery, the arcades, the haunted house and iconic boardwalk eateries where city birds flock. You will also experience the OC nightlife through the eyes of Tommy Vann of Tommy Vann and the Echoes.

Many of us vacationing in Ocean City look upon the boardwalk as the main thoroughfare of the resort. We have to cross the boardwalk on our way to the beach in the morning to save our spot for the day. As we do, we might have to dodge those travelling on the boards via bike. During the season when Ocean City experiences a twenty-fold growth in population, one is free to ride a bike until 10:00 am on the boardwalk. Of course, some of those riders only ride on a bike during their OC vacation, so that journey across the boards could be dicey.

2020 Kitefest
from balcony of Lankford
Photo by Eugene Marshall

As a frequently travelled walkway, the boards also connect us to eats, souvenirs and amusements throughout the day. For those walking the entire span, wooden benches line the route for a quick or not-so-quick chance to get off of one's feet for a while. Within the last 20 years or so, these benches also make for some interesting reading as well. The resort invites everyone for a fee to attach a memorial plaque to the favorite perch of Grandmom and Grandpa. Many names become familiar, especially if you stay at the same hotel or condominium year after year.

Michael Morgan describes the boardwalk's beginnings:

> With so much growth, wooden walkways were built between the new structures to make it easier to walk across the sand. The wooden walkways gave Ocean City the appearance of a town out of

The Boardwalk at 8th Street
Photo by Ellen Marshall

the Old West, and on the ocean side the resort adopted an idea that had originated in Merry Old England. Long before Ocean City was established, vacationers in Great Britain travelled to the ports on the English Channel, where they spent their day watching the steady parade of passing ships. At some of the channel ports, wide wooden walkways were erected to enable visitors to get a better view of the steamboats, sailing ships and other passing vessels. By the time that Ocean City had developed into a resort, these boardwalks had become a standard feature at most seaside towns...

In the early days the boardwalk was put down in sections so that it could be taken up at the end of the summer and stored to prevent damage from winter storms...[16]

The boardwalk at Ocean City from its humble beginnings in 1902 became the "place to be seen." Lovely ladies in flowing boot length skirts strolled arm-in-arm with their equally well-dressed mates in the pre-World War I era. The boardwalk was elevated at that time and I suppose one could catch a quick smooch from his beloved. Couples were sheltered from public view as they walked under the elevated boards.

It appears from historical accounts that bathing in the Ocean was only for the most fit. Photographs from the time show bloomer-clad ladies clinging to a rope when walking into the surf. If there was frolicking in the waves, it was only as a precursor to the shower and change before going onto the boardwalk. Bath houses along the boardwalk provided water and some privacy. Some were even pushed down the boardwalk in large adult-sized strollers or chairs. They were described as "Three-wheeled wicker chairs, which could be rented for fifty cents an hour."[17] Then strolling the boardwalk was like a promenade on the Champs Élysée, Paris – one did it as a highlight of the day, often before dinner.

A dramatic event, the hurricane of 1933, though devastating to many existing structures, impacted the resort forever. Eben Davis and Damon Talbot describe its effects:

> The storm's greatest and most lasting impact was a 50-foot wide, 8-foot deep inlet, that was carved through the barrier island by a continuous four day ebb tide, flowing from the bay out to the ocean. Three entire streets were submerged at the south end of the town... This inlet made Ocean City the state's only Atlantic port. The resulting commercial and sport fishing boom greatly shaped the character of the Ocean City we know today, as vacationers content with more modest accommodations flocked in large numbers to crab and fish, and dozens of hotels and restaurants sprang up to meet their needs.[18]

When the jetty was formed in 1933, the sand began to build up along the beach. Eventually the boardwalk was at its beginnings raised high enough for horses to ride under. It became level with the beach in the 1930s.

Ocean City's boardwalk is like the town center of any destination. It is where tourists and residents stroll to pick up a pizza, walk the dog, bike, take in the amusements or shop for souvenirs. I recall many a summer vacation when we would actually meet families from home on the boards. Some va-

The Boardwalk Tram takes visitors from 28th Street to inlet
Photo by Eugene Marshall

cationers enjoy "people watching" from their perches on the boardwalk benches. One might not know the individuals they see on the boards, but they know that they are all enjoying the boardwalk together at the same time. Multiply that event by an average of 850,000+ visitors each year since 1962 and our shared experience has been enjoyed by over 14, 250,000 souls.

Strolling along the boardwalk happens anytime from the early pre-dawn hours until 10:00 am. It continues until the crowds come from dinner time and last through the night. If you stay at a hotel, condo or apartment below 9th Street, most likely your journey is all on foot. Those spending their time at OC further up the boards have the option of driving, taking the Ocean City bus or the boardwalk tram. It is rare for a family vacationing there to skip the boardwalk. It is integral to the experience of the resort. For that reason, real estate and business opportunities along the 2½ mile stretch are prime properties. As they say "Hot, hot, hot."

So, what should a new visitor to Ocean City expect of the boardwalk? How does it feel during season and other times?

Today's Ocean City visitors can expect that the temperature typically varies from 29° F to 84°F[19] ... most of the year. Even when the August mid-day sun is beating down upon the sand, the sunbathers and the joggers, it is not unusual for a sudden wind and breeze to moderate the heat for a time.

When one leaves the boardwalk to go for a swim, beach umbrellas placed a bit to break a sudden wind gust and stay in its place are a necessity. Naturally sunscreen with an SPF rating is recommended to use all day. Those cloudy day sunburns happen more than one would think.

Back to the boardwalk... Watching the modern Ocean City visitor, I see clothing ranging the gamut from the fashion- conscious desiring to show off their new tans to the long cotton maxi dress to shorts and tees and, finally the bikini-clad young woman dashing for a quick bite. That is like most beach communities world-wide, I imagine. What is unique about Ocean City is that few really care. There used to be a town ordinance requiring a cover-up over a bathing suit. If that still is on the books, it is rarely enforced.

For several years the Ocean City leaders, their tourism personnel and businesspersons have aspired to expand the season to include spring and late fall events. Boardwalk businesses and the larger hotels operate on a longer schedule to that end. Even the smaller gift shops will open on weekends so that the boardwalk crowd can do some browsing and some spending.

Those of us who love Ocean City and live close enough are taking advantage of the other months beyond summer. We

Vintage postcard of the Idylwilde showing the old boardwalk

come down three or four times in fall, winter and mid-spring just to enjoy the view from an ocean front balcony. Many prefer to be at the ocean and on the boardwalk during those slow times. Residents tell me that although they depend on the business that the traditional season brings, it is a refreshing change to go back to a more leisurely pace. It is a time to reclaim their solitude.

With Ocean City development came the beginnings of the boardwalk as an entertainment and shopping venue. The first wave of tourist attractions after the rise of historic hotels was the construction of the pier pavilion in 1907. It "...contained a dance hall (The Pier Ballroom), a skating rink, bowling alley, pool tables and assorted refreshment booths."[20]

After the construction of a new highway bridge in 1916 which entered the island at Worcester Street, the completion of Ritchie Highway (Route 2) in 1938 and the opening of the first span of the Bay Bridge in 1952, travel to Ocean City became much quicker and easier. Many more vacationers started to travel to the Maryland resort. This ended the illusion that Delaware and New Jersey beaches were more attractive. Along with this new discovery of what was to become an iconic beach town, the beginning of a business and building boom took hold. Soon-to-be shopkeepers heard the second call and lined the boardwalk with their variety stores, some of which are still standing today.

The first mall on the boardwalk was erected in the 1950s on the boardwalk at 9th Street. It contained Hess Apparel, The Embers Restaurant, an auction gallery, a Candy Kitchen, a gift shop and an Alaska stand. Prior to those shops, the Beach Club was a hangout for young people. Next to the club, a guy and his date could get a snack at Tom Shill's Hamburger Heaven.

The clock on the beach side of the boardwalk, next to the public bathrooms, was a focal point for sun bathers. Anytime one arose from a sand nap, he or she could look up towards the clock to determine the hour. 9th street also became a gathering place for teens when a video arcade was opened.

An ad from the 1956 describes Hess Apparel and other OC attractions:

Walking the Boards with Grandmom
Photo by Eugene Marshall

Santa Maria, a new ocean front motor hotel invites you to eat at the Captain's Table, buy clothes at Hess Apparel, Boardwalk at 9th; Pete's Chicken Koop at Phila. Ave. at 4th St. will give you a complete Delmarvalous fried chicken dinner for $2.25, flowers are found at Burton's; fishing equipment at Schafer's swordfish basin; rent a bike at Todd's Bicycle Shop; dance to the music of Hank Clausen at the Inlet Casino (*Salisbury Times*, August 3, 1956).[21]

Where'd You Get That Cute Swimsuit?

In between the Roosevelt Hotel and the Plimhimmon, what is now the Plim Plaza between Division and 2nd Streets, stood Edwards 5 & 10¢ Store. It was an often photographed beachfront general store. Edwards opened its doors in 1937. You could buy just about anything there from souvenirs or beach chairs to beach clothing. By the 1970s some late summer visitors planned their vacation to coincide with Edwards "end-of-season" sale. That terrific beach umbrella you hesitated to pick up at full price was marked down about 40-50% of its June cost. Well worth the trip!

Edwards was originally named Edward's 5 & 10. It is a destination for many boardwalk strollers. You could either browse the collections in the gift aisles or buy that yearly souvenir, a reminder of summer's visit or a gift for the dog sitter. As with many Ocean City businesses, Edwards employed seasonal help to ring the register from May to September.

I shopped at Edwards often, almost every time we travelled to Ocean City. Edwards was a great place to shop during their end-of-season sale. I could pick up t-shirts for the kids or swimsuits and a nice memento for my mother. When I ascended the steps to the second floor, I could find wind chimes and beach toys at bargain prices. The checkout line was deep during this sale, signaling that many of us enjoyed the same ritual.

Bill Gibbs,[22] owner of Dough Roller, bought the property in 1980. Edwards began to share its two-story display space with Quiet Storm, an up market surf shop. During the off-season of 2012-13, the entire space was devoted to Quiet Storm and Edwards opened as a smaller boardwalk front store selling beach clothing only. Edwards is still owned by the Gibbs family.

The official summer season at Ocean City, like other resort towns on the East Coast, begins Memorial Day weekend and runs through Labor Day weekend. During the off-season,

Plaque designating the former site of Edwards 5 & 10

many boardwalk stores open on holiday weekends and for Springfest, first Thursday through Sunday in May, and Sunfest, 3rd weekend in September. Most of the summer workers are high school and college kids. However, since they often have to leave Ocean City to go back to school in late August, the stores, restaurants and hotels supplement their staffing with international college students. From the late 1990s, Ocean City has employed students from Western Europe, mainly Ireland and Scotland, and from eastern Europe, notably the Czech Republic, Romania, Kosova, Albania, and Russia.

Ovie, a former student from Romania, is one who stayed in the U.S. after working a summer. I spoke to him at the Sunsations at 9th Street and he told me he has been here 12 years, is married and has two children.

Other stores followed Edwards' boardwalk presence. Jewelry stores can be spotted several places along the beachfront from the inlet to 28th Street. Park Place Jewelers, founded in 1996 as Michael's Jewelry on 5th and the boards by Todd Ferrante now sits between 2nd and 3rd Streets. The store features special beach jewelry in gold and silver by designers such as OJ Hook and Pandora. Mark Douglas jewelry store has several locations. Sanibal Jewelry on the inlet pier and the boardwalk includes costume jewelry with beach themes. All are great places to find after season designer jewelry specials up to 50% off. Such establishments bring a bit of ocean-themed bling to the boardwalk shopper. Some shoppers will spend more than what the usual souvenirs of coffee mugs and sand turtles would cost. Those 50% off signs tempt lovers to pop the big question.

Another historical shop, Townsend's Washington Pharmacy, was at Somerset Street. Founded by Dr. Townsend in

1930. In 1925 many of the surrounding buildings burned in a major fire. Michael Morgan writes:

> Soon flames could be seen leaping out of the Atlantic Hotel. An eyewitness recalled "The fire just kept blazing away. It burned the electric light plant, then it skipped across the street (the boardwalk at that time was known as Atlantic Avenue)and burned the laundry at the Atlantic Hotel and it burned the whole Atlantic Hotel and some buildings on Wicomico Street."... Anne...Bunting and another dozen women snatched bed sheets from their homes and descended on the pharmacy, which was the resorts principal source of medicines. After each sheet was filled with a pile of bottles, boxes and drugs, they were dragged to safety.[23]

Townsend's survived the fire. In the years that followed several pharmacies served the residents of Ocean City. Bailey's Pharmacy at 8th Street and Baltimore Avenue was open until 2012. At Bailey's one could stock up on medicines, suntan lotion and disposable kitchenware. Other national chain drugstores like Rite Aid, Walgreens and CVS were late 20th century additions to the resort. But today no pharmacy has a boardwalk presence.

The Kite Loft

I walk into this gem at 5th and the boards and become a kid again. First, the whirly gigs and the multi-colored flags make me want to touch and play with them. As I walk into the store, I hear one of my favorite sounds, the tring-a-ling of wind chimes. I am enchanted.

Bill "King of the Wind" Ochse opened shop in 1978. Their website offers amazing tips for kite flyers like "How to Fly Kites," "Kiting Records" and "Wind Strengths." Bill knew all he had to do was fly some kites along the beach in front and the customers would flock in. Jay and Mary Lynn Knerr are the current owners.

The Kite Loft hosts an international kite festival each fall during Sunfest, the third weekend after Labor Day. Professional Kiters from all over the country launch beautifully crafted kites and compete in various categories.

The P.T. Barnum of the Art World

From the time a first time visitor to Ocean City walks the boards approaching from Third or First Street, a slightly a-kilter, totally inviting, store facade pops into view. Signs are hanging off the exterior, weird messages invite you in, artwork jumps up at you. Welcome to the Ocean Gallery at 2nd Street.

Joe Kro-Art,[24] its founder, is described as "the PT Barnum of Fine Art" by the Sunny Day Guide. Open all year round, the Ocean Gallery is a fun place to browse through with its three floors of wall-to-wall posters, vintage photos and many genres of paintings. Some of it would be considered "high art." Aubrey Bodine, as well as August Renoir and Toulouse Lautrec hang around. It is also here that local artists, such as Paul DeRemegis from Baltimore and Paul McGee of Virginia, exhibit and sign their works for Ocean City visitors and natives.

Joe, sometimes pensive, always engaging, is most proud that his art enterprise makes people smile. "It's worth it, just to watch the smiles and grins as people walk from the boardwalk. That's why I do this, why I stand at the register near the entrance. I love to watch the young and not-as-young – the delight in their eyes."

Joseph Leonard Kro-Art, Jr. didn't think his scholarship to Maryland Institute College of Art in Baltimore at age 8 was worth pursuing. As his website explains:

> However, as much as he enjoyed drawing and painting, KroArt couldn't stand taking art courses! The formality and static nature of art instruction made him uncomfortable, and the energy and excitement that he had always associated with art was suddenly missing. It was then that he realized that for him, art should NOT be experienced in this fashion, and he promised himself that he would always strive to keep the FUN in art!

So, Joe packed up his car with some of his work and left his Baltimore City home, intent on selling his work on the Ocean City boardwalk. He spent summers during his years at Towson State University at the Ocean peddling his artistic wares. Then Mr. Kro-Art taught high school for seven years in a Baltimore City school, only to have that yearning to return to the art world gnawing at him. In 1974 he founded Ocean Gallery and later his adult sons joined him in the venture of "keeping the fun in art."[25]

During an interview Joe described his vision for the Ocean gallery in these words:

> "My highest hope for ocean gallery is expanding exponentially every day!!! Being featured in publications and 2 new major motion pictures this year is truly ASTOUNDING!!!!!!!"[26]

Ocean Gallery – Keeping the fun in art
Photo by Eugene Marshall

Please, Mom, can I get on the Merry-go-Round?

Towards the end of the boardwalk between the Inlet and Somerset Street sits a multi- acre spread of fun called Trimper's Amusement Park. Daniel Trimper and his wife, both immigrants from Germany, opened the vintage amusement park in 1892. They originally named it Windsor Resort and then Luna Park. Remnants of the historic hotel can be spotted behind the present Haunted House.

The *piece de resistance* in the Trimper Pavilion is the vintage carousel. Imagine the face of any six year old lit with glee when the child enters the pavilion where the merry-go-round resides. "Mommy, mommy, I want to go on the pretty horsey," echoes throughout this land of fantasy. The lovely organ music as it plays in oompapa staccato, the motion of the animals as they ride up and down, the reflections of riders as they glide past the mirrors, the scores of parents lined-up to take pictures of their children's delight – all this happens every day of the summer season many times over.

Now, think about all of the sixty year-olds, reliving that first ride with a childhood friend or sibling. It is pure magic that this gorgeous work of art and fun continues to amaze. Visitors see that some of the animals rock, some slide up and down a pole, others stand proudly. Besides the carefully crafted horses, there is a frog, a stork, a few ornate benches, one with Mr. Toad. In all, the carousel contains 12 jumping horses, 11 standing horse, 25 menagerie animals, and 4 chariots. In 1996, the Hershell-Spillman 1902 carousel received the National Carousel Association's Historical Carousel Award.[27]

Dolores Monet, describing the most beautiful addition to the park, writes on her website:

> In 1912 the Trimpers purchased a Hershell-Spillman carousel. Build[sic] in 1902, the beautiful carousel featured a hand carved menagerie and is, today, the oldest continually running carousel in the USA...

When Gordon Katz was researching the carousel for his book, he discovered that the carousel was actually built in 1912.[28]

The Trimper's building contains other vintage kiddie rides like the 1920s- era small carousel, the caged ferris wheel perfect for toddlers and their older brothers, a whip, fire engine ride and the boat ride round a shallow moat. Adults can partake of the daredevil fun of the bumper cars.

One of the highlights of my Ocean City vacations was Trimpers. When I graduated to the older kids rides, I walked out of the back of the pavilion and found an amusement

Trimper Vintage Carousel on the boardwalk of Ocean City
Photo by Ellen Marshall

park that offered what seemed like everything. Sometimes my parents could afford a string of ride tickets to go on a spring-loaded rollercoaster, The Shock Wave. I could giggle till I get dizzy on the Tilt-a-Whirl, or race along an undulating ramp to pop or rock music, complete with a deejay on the Himalaya or The Matterhorn.

My brothers, Carl and Jerry, played the carnival-like games of chance to win a stuffed animal. If we turned the corner we could shoot a pop rifle in a wild west saloon, circa 1890. Carl could test his hand-sight coordination and hit the hat of the old cowboy clanging the keys on a piano or catch the frog jumping over the pond. Hey, wait, weren't we inside a clapboard drinking establishment? Fantasy fools, no rules, again.

We would often meet friends and family sharing vacation weeks at night at the Trimper park or the pier rides. The pier amusements appeal to older teens and adults because the park boasts thrill rides like swings that throw you out over the Atlantic Ocean. A giant ferris wheel stands at 110 feet high and can hold 144 riders during the peak occupancy month of August. Recently the ferris wheel is illuminated with a light show that delights our grandsons at night. And the Pirate Ship brings out the screams like any time one watches Alfred Hitchcock's birds line up on that telephone wire and monkey bars.

A short trip down the boards, in between the souvenir shop and the carney games, an eerie recorded laugh and a somewhat ramshackle spooky front invites one to ride the tram inside the Haunted House. There you ride through cobwebs, ghosts flying out, shipwrecked sailors come alive – all designed to scare the bejesus out of young and old alike. Before the present haunting, the Lloyd Jester family owned and operated a major boardwalk attraction, Laughing Sal.

Jake Fewster, writing for *The Baltimore Sun*, tells us about the creator of the Trimper Funhouse:

> Built in 1964, this frightful house is an important part of the legacy of Bill Tracy, master of amusement park horror...The house is an important part of the legacy of Bill Tracy, master of dark rides, those amusement park staples that ferry patrons through interiors where lighting, sound and creative displays are designed to amuse — or terrify.
>
> Tracy made his career terrifying customers. He started with Ringling Bros. and Barnum & Bailey

circus in the early 1950s and gained notoriety after designing floats for the Macy's Thanksgiving Day Parade.[29]

Laughing Sal, who appears as the heroine in John Barth's *Lost in the Funhouse,* is spending her genteel retirement years encased on the second floor of the Ocean City Lifesaving Museum. One can still hear her contagious laugh. Barth writes:

> Larger than life. Fat Mary mechanically shook, rocked on her heels, slapped her thighs while recorded laughter – uproarious, female- came amplified from a hidden loudspeaker. It chuckled, wheezed, wept: turned in vain to catch its breath: tittered, groaned, exploded raucous and anew. You couldn't hear it without laughing yourself no matter how you felt.[30]

In the early 20th century, the Ocean City Pier, built in 1907, provided more genteel entertainment. The pier supported a pavilion in which there was "a dance hall, a skating rink, bowling alleys, pool tables and assorted refreshment booths." In those early days, walking the boardwalk was a way to see who was there for the rest the resort promised. A fire destroyed the original pier structure in 1994.

A commenter on Dolores Monet's hub pages, kittythedreamer, resonates with many an Ocean City visitor:

> voted up and awesome, dolores! i went to ocean city as a kid and also for my senior week out of high school. always loved the boardwalk…most people don't realize how big it actually is. . thanks for putting up the history of maryland's (sic) atlantic treasure. :) [31]

Ding, ding, ding, ding. Can't you hear in your memory's ear the sound of the winning at Skeeball in Marty's Playland at Worchester Street? And can't you see the neon sign that shouts come in for a while, kids of all ages? The historic arcade houses skeeball lanes and miniature cranes at Diggerville that have been around for a century. The gypsy woman who draws you to her glass and wooden booth has been handing out fortunes for over 50 years. These vintage attractions live alongside the more recent arcade games of Donkey Kong and NBA Basketball.

The cacophony of the various video games and pinball machines create a symphony of delight to Ocean City fun seekers. Who doesn't want a chance to compete for the tickets which can then be redeemed for prizes? Over the course of a week's vacation, one could rack up a significant amount of game tickets. Children would ponder for hours over the tempting display of portable radios, stuffed animals, dolls, cowboy regalia, flashlights and toy cars, trying to decide what to redeem their winning tickets on? Decisions, decisions.

Gypsy Woman at Marty's Playland
Reprinted by permission of Dolores Monet

Can't Have Enough of Dem Crabs

When the stomach starts to signal "feed me," Ocean

City offers several iconic eating places on the boardwalk. A quick glance at any of the beach newspapers – *The Dispatch/Maryland Coast Dispatch, The Beachcomb, Ocean City Today* – reminds the reader of the many restaurants in Ocean City. Some of these eateries rise to the level of gotta-go every time in many OC visitors' estimations.

Take, for example, Thrashers Boardwalk Fries. Ocean City gives a visitor so many eatery choices, 200 plus, to be exact. Restaurants unique to Ocean City keep families coming back each year. Like other destinations, there are "must-do" places to eat while there. Walk onto the boardwalk and you immediately catch a whiff of Thrasher's fries, seasoned as they have been for decades, with vinegar and salt. Or the frying onions at Bull on the Beach meet your nose as you walk and your ears anticipate the crackle. All you have to do is step out of your hotel and whish, umpteen delicious aromas compete for your attention. How do they do that? You are almost tempted to look for the behind-the-scenes fan which blows those tempting smells onto the boards.

Let's allow our noses to take us on a culinary journey on the Ocean City boardwalk. First, we stop at 8th Street. The delicious smell brings a long line during the summer season. In 1929 a Georgian known as Mr. J.T. Thrasher thought it would be a good idea to sell only one food, french fries, from his food stand. According to the Thrasher website, "His idea? Simply to produce the best tasting French fry ever eaten - past, present or future. He did."

J.T. Thrasher of Georgia founded this venerable fry stand in 1929, vowing to concentrate on making one food very well. He employed young girls from a Christian-affiliated school in Georgia to help run the business. The girls were housed in

Dolles Saltwater Taffy circa 1930
Photo courtesy of Anna Bushnell Dolle

a dormitory over the present Bank of Ocean City. His first Thrasher's was at the pier and, when he sold the business to Franklin "Crip" Hastings in 1974, another location was opened at 2nd Street and the Boardwalk. Mr. Hastings kept to the original recipe.

Eighty-four years later Thrasher's French Fries continues to be one of the treats vacationers keep coming back for. Smell that salt and vinegar seasoning at another boardwalk location, 8th Street. Bet you'll buy some.

Thrasher's has three locations on the boards – at the pier, on 2nd, and at 8th. One might suppose that the original goal was realized, because on any given summer day the lines form 40+ deep at the pier. And it is worth the wait. Something about the blend of the vinegar, the salt, and the oil makes a

Current Photo of Thrasher's sign
Photo by Eugene Marshall

visitor start salivating.

As one Thrasher's aficionado, Andrea Bowland, observes:

> Nearly every visitor who makes an annual pilgrimage to the seaside resort [Ocean City, MD] has to make at least one stop at the famous boardwalk... with the wind and salty ocean air behind your back. Or maybe it's the food: saltwater taffy, chocolates, popcorn, chili dogs, snow cones, or the most famous treat of all, Thrasher's French Fries.[32]

The venerable boardwalk establishment combines just four simple ingredients: potatoes, peanut oil, apple cider vinegar, and salt potatoes, peanut oil, apple cider vinegar, and salt.

Bowland continues that their fries' ingredients turn

> into a treat that has practically come to be as representative of the boardwalk, as the boardwalk itself.

The two are nearly synonymous with one another.[33]

Andrea continues:

> There's a man who holds court in a small white stand on the Ocean City boardwalk, nearly every day, while the weather is nice. He oversees your vacation, watches your children's eager faces, and hands out the boardwalk's most coveted food. He makes sure that the famous potatoes uphold the integrity of the original recipe started in 1929. He is Les Morris, commonly known amongst his co-workers, as "Lord of the Fries" at the infamous boardwalk staple, Thrasher's Fries.
>
> Les doesn't own Thrasher's. That distinction belongs to Buddy Jenkins and the Boardwalk Hotel Group. But it's a safe bet that Les knows his way around a French fry better than anybody. He's worked there for 34 years. When asked about the often copied, but never quite duplicated flavor of Thrasher's, and its distinction of only serving salt and vinegar as toppings, Les says simply, "Well that's the way it's always been done."[34]

Candy Kitchen

Candy Kitchen opened its doors in 1937 to sell saltwater taffy. Lynn Bartlett writes on his blog:

> Recently a bit of nostalgia and a big craving for something sweet and gooey drove me to stop at the familiar white painted shop front with the raspberry colored, circular logo which has become

a tradition for folks visiting Ocean City Maryland for 70 years...Candy Kitchen! Long known for the best homemade salt-water taffy (love those flavors) and fudge...[35]

Candy Kitchen opened a store on 9th Street and the Boardwalk and it soon became one of the places to hang out with your friends. Besides the store's taffy, the chain began to offer make-your-own ice cream sundaes. This popular summer treat starts with your choice of ice cream flavors, two or three dips if you brought enough money. From that station you go to the "fixins" bar. Load up on hot fudge and caramel before the coconut, nuts, chocolate sprinkles, and assorted candy bar bits pile on. Then, of course, more hot fudge. If you are really feeling decadent, add some whipped cream and hope you don't have to share with your younger sister.

Candy Kitchen has become a must-go place for our young grandsons. They have evolved with the times and feature Lego brick-shaped sweets, all types of gummies and stuffed toys of popular tv characters. The owners hit upon a genius marketing strategy, since these are all placed about eye level.

Dolle's

To continue this olfactory trip down the boardwalk, let us walk to Dolle's, where our eyes can feast on the saltwater taffy and the array of chocolates and jelly candies. Soon our nose follows to the long queue for candy popcorn. Caramel, nuts, corn – the smells that lengthen the line, along with the *pop, pop, popping* the patrons hear coming from behind the window. If the popcorn is not enough to satisfy, we can walk inside the store to be tempted by rows and rows of chocolate confections.

Dolle's has enticed OC visitors since 1910. Dolle's stands on the boardwalk and Wicomico Street and was founded by Rudolph and Amelia Dolle four years after they visited the resort from their home in New York. Their first venture on the site was Rudolph's hand carved family carousel. But then the saltwater taffy business next door became available and they bought it.

> ...back then, the saltwater taffy was cooked in small copper kettles, cooled on marble slabs, and pulled by hand on large hooks. It was cut into small pieces with scissors and then wrapped by hand in wax paper. The cost: 37¢ per pound or three pounds for one dollar! Over the years the manufacturing process has changed dramatically. The candy is now cooked in large copper kettles and cooled on stainless steel, water jacketed tables. It is then machine pulled and wrapped on high speed wrapping machines which produce up to 650 pieces per minute![36]

Early theme-park entertainment pioneer Daniel Trimper convinced Mr. Dolle, who was a noted carousel artisan, to build and set up a carousel at Wicomico Street in 1893. So, the Dolles began what was to become more than a century of business growth in the new resort community. Anna Dolle Bushnell recounts,[37] "In front of the property," was a little man who owned a cart from which he sold taffy. Soon my great grandfather bought out the cart vendor, the carousel was victim to a fire in 1925. They decided not to rebuild the carousel, but to sell saltwater taffy and other confectionary, by then bringing their son into the business,"[38] Ms. Dolle

Dolle's circa 1928 colorized
Photo courtesy of Anna Bushnell Dolle

Bushnell states. Dolle cooks the chocolate fudge every morning and loves doing so. Anna and her brother, Andrew, began running the family business in 2000.

The Dolles, like so many other early Ocean City business families, dedicated their lives and family's future to building up a thriving resort. Anna is proud of the fact that the advent of e-sales and social media has made Dolle's products available across the world. "Dolle's is part of the make-up of Ocean City; so much about Maryland pride and Maryland-made products," Anna proudly asserts.

Seaside resorts feature this confectionary treat and market its contents as a great souvenir for those who want a nostalgic taste of the ocean when they return home. The ingredients for saltwater taffy include:

- 2 cups sugar
- 2 tablespoons cornstarch

- 1 cup light corn syrup
- 2 teaspoons glycerin (optional)
- 3/4 cup water
- 2 tablespoons butter
- 1 teaspoon salt
- 1/4 to 1 teaspoon flavoring (such as vanilla, lemon, maple, or mint)
- 3 drops food coloring (optional)

Note, no salt water is included, but it does require some pulling muscle.

Wockenfuss Candy

Still have not satisfied your beach sweet tooth? Stop in at Wockenfuss, a Baltimore-based candy store founded by the Wockenfuss family in the Gardenville neighborhood in 1915. From candy apples to fudge to jellied treats, the tempting multi-colored displays (see photo below) have drawn beach-goers in for a quick treat or a tastebud memory to take home.

Wockenfuss Candy has always been a go-to place in the neighborhood where I grew up. We always went to the Belair Road store in the 4500 block of Belair Road for Christmas stockings, Valentine sweets, Easter baskets, and other special occasions. Herman Charles Wockenfuss came to Baltimore from West Prussia, Germany in 1875. At that time many German families had settled in Gardenville in Baltimore City. The 106-year-old company expanded to eight locations, 2 in Ocean City. The business is still operated by its 4th generation of Wockenfusses.[39]

How delighted we were when they opened a store at the Boardwalk and 1st. They also have a store on Ocean Gate-

Wockenfuss Candy at Boardwalk and 1st Street
Photo by Eugene Marshall

way, Route 50. Many more families can now grow up loving Wockenfuss treats.

Pizza

Pizza – who doesn't eat pizza at Ocean City? Vacation is no time for low-carb dieting, and Ocean City offers many varieties of this American favorite. The Dough Roller, at the boardwalk and 3rd Street, began making pizza in 1980, and millions have flocked there since. Tables inside can accommodate Mom, Dad, Grandmom, Baby Tina, and her five siblings with ease.

The Dough Roller website explains Bill Gibbs' motivation for opening their restaurant:

> Bill Gibbs, a lifelong Ocean City resident, began his working life as a beach umbrella vendor for then Breakers Hotel owner, Mrs. Timmons. As he sat

on the beach near the boardwalk, Bill recalls many tourists asking where they could eat lunch. That barrage of the same question haunted him until he could do something to fill the void, start his own restaurant chain, The DoughRoller, in the hotel for which he once schlepped beach umbrellas.[40]

Their first change was to replace the large front porch with a pizza restaurant, The Dough Roller. Mr. Gibbs recalled that some people lamented the loss of a porch, while he saw it as an opportunity to enter the resort's restaurant business sorely lacking a lot of casual dining places on the boardwalk.

Bill and Julie Gibbs built a pizza empire from that initial investment. Carrying on the tradition of taking big risks for potential gains, the Gibbs banked on a beach crowd craving pizza. Their locations prove the gamble paid off.

Tony's Pizza, another boardwalk fixture, has been serving mounds of mozzarella on pepperoni to millions of vacationers. The restaurant sits very close to the boardwalk front of the Atlantic Hotel, the first hotel in Ocean City. Tony's is also close to Marty's Playland, within earshot of the music and clanging of the arcade games. So, it's a convenient spot to grab a quick and inexpensive lunch or dinner between boardwalk entertainments.

Tony's also has a second-story rooftop dining area. From this vantage point, diners can take in all of the people watching below. It almost has the feel of a Bourbon Street second-floor restaurant, and the people noise can be as persistent as that in New Orleans.

After dinner, the young and not-so-young adults who want to dance the night away, and perhaps be photographed

Breakers Hotel circa 1940
The Dough Roller replaced the porch shown here.

for one of the beach weeklies, travel to one of several clubs. While the original dancing was done on the old pier, crowds migrated to other venues, many of them on Philadelphia Avenue or Coastal Highway and along the Sinepuxent Bay.

In the 1940s, Dr. Francis J. Townsend built a bandstand at Somerset Street. Frank Sacca, father of Nancy Sacca,[41] led the Ocean City Community Band in summer concerts. At the Pier's Ballroom, "Many residents and visitors fondly recall the dances ...and dancing to music by big band celebrities like Benny Goodman, Glen Miller, Jimmy Dorsey, and Harry James."[42]

Denise McDermott waxes poetic about her youth working at Ocean City:

> On my day off, I would go with the girls up the coast to where the dunes were (around where condo row now is), to get out of town and onto the

beach, away from the crowds. Or we'd go to Trader Lee's for a bottle of thick, rich chocolate milk, and then on to Salisbury, via as many back roads as we could possibly find, to our ultimate destination of the Park, where we would swing on the swing sets, or just talk and relax our day away. In the pier building, where Ripley's Believe It or Not, is now housed, was still holding dances back in 1970. I actually got to dance on that old Pier Ballroom floor, but it was to the new beat of rock and roll. What fun it was!! Oh how I wish we had a grand space like that, now that I enjoy real Ballroom Dancing![43] (sic)

However, this boardwalk fun was not accessible to persons of color until 1965. Although many citizens of color worked in the hotels and restaurants, they were precluded from enjoying the beach and boardwalk except for one day a year. There were separate rooming houses for blacks, at Henry's Colored Hotel for the waiters and head chefs who worked at the resort. And "only a select few blacks were allowed to live on the island proper."[44]

From the 1940s until the Public Accommodations Law became the law of the land, two days in the week after Labor Day would be set aside as "Colored Day." People of color were allowed on the beach and the boardwalk for those days only. Dona Ang Yates recalls "My mother and I would sneak under the boardwalk so we could listen to the music..."[45] Dona saw this as their way to secretly enjoy music they enjoyed while seeming to comply with the social mores.

I found it interesting that several of my interviewees, like

Tommy Vann and the Echoes
Photo Courtesy of Tommy Vann Productions

Dona, openly recount the past racial discrimination policies in their city's history. It is a snapshot of a time in Maryland and throughout the country when people of color were excluded from experiences that whites took for granted. One of my conversations during research told about how a woman's family's black nanny who would have to room downstairs with the hotel's staff in the 1950s and 1960s.

As the resort expanded, many businesses chose to build on the bayside of Ocean City. Real estate was less expensive and more plentiful, and there was ample space for parking. Among these businesses were the clubs, and one of the most popular was the Ship's Cafe.

Pete Bonis, the founder of the Ship's Cafe Marina, like many Ocean City residents and visitors, was a world-renowned marlin fisherman. "His marina and tournaments kept the marlin industry thriving in the 1960s and '70s, and his

Ship's Cafe restaurant was a favorite of visiting celebrities."[46]

Tommy Vann, headliner of Tommy Vann and the Echoes in the 1960s and 1970s, recalls the Ocean City club scene of that time. Tommy's band performed at the Ship's Cafe, on 14th Street and the Bay. The entire enterprise consisted of a restaurant seating 400, a motel, and a marina.

Tommy captures the era in these words:

> We entertained during the summers from 1972-1977...The crowds were very diversified, young and old... we worked the inside first, then in the gazebo area...they all had a good time...and we had a lot of people who followed us. For instance, I remember the Budweiser, Anheuser-Busch yacht, would come into Ocean City and dock the yacht at the marina of the Ship's Café...they'd all come in and the Busch family would have a great time ... Frank Perdue (Poultry King of the Eastern Shore) would come often ...we were graced with a lot of celebrities.

The Whip and Ferris Wheel
Ocean City, MD

Where We Stay

"If I read a book and it makes my whole body so cold no fire can ever warm me, I know that it is poetry."

Emily Dickinson

Coming out of King's Cottages are Dolores Sprissler, Kerri Leslie and Nicole Marshall Slomba. Marshall family photo.

Clapboard houses, quirky first-floor apartments and Victorian style hotels are what make Ocean City a picture postcard place to sun and fun. The resort changed dramatically from the late 1930s through the building boom of the 60s and 70s. Each year, the summer population grows and those 320,000-345,000[47] need a place to stay overnight.

Families who come down to the Ocean each year know their temporary landlords' first names. They often keep in touch during the winter months. Hotel owners could count on that generation and the two following to return every year. Often they would come during the same week to their establishments with families in tow. Going to Ocean City became a tradition, loved and never-missed – Christmas in July.

Ms. Carrie owned King's Cottages between 6th and 7th on

Baltimore Avenue. She was delighted each year we returned and marveled at how much our three children had grown. Like so many young families who returned every year and often the same week, we ticked off the summer calendar to the exact date we would return to "Miss Carrie's home." Miss Carrie and her husband lived in the cottage facing Baltimore Avenue. We stayed in one of the two cottages abutting the alley between Baltimore and the Boardwalk. During our week we made it feel as much our home as hers. But the distinct smell of salt water and fig trees told us it was ours for just a while.

King's Cottages had ample space for a family of 5. From the street level, we walked into a living room/dining room that led to the kitchen. Three small bedrooms and full bath completed the space. Its décor, like many of the older hotels, was mid-century basic, but it was comfortable for our family to rent for a week. The draw for me was the wonderful beachy scent that came for free. We brought down our linens and Miss Carrie provided cookware, dishes, and flatware.

Miss Carrie followed in the tradition of the early owners at what became known as 'The Ladies' Resort," women who ran the earliest hotels and rooming houses.

Hotels that began as small rooming houses with visionaries and risk-takers at their front desks became thriving enterprises over those 50 years of tremendous growth. Vacationers along the eastern seaboard were drawn to Ocean City as a family resort. This chapter chronicles how a $25 per-lot investment in 1884 led to a multi-million dollar fortune in real estate. These pioneers' goal to comfortably house a summer population with modest means created a thriving hospitality industry.

Stories told by and about these pioneering hotel families give an inside perspective of how the resort's hotel industry grew. Their lives and business decisions are so rich in detail that they paint a picture of what it takes to be successful in a beach resort town.

Two major events spurred the development of the land between the Sinepuxent Bay and the Atlantic Ocean into a thriving beach town. The first was the expansion of the railroad in 1876. The second event was the construction of the Chesapeake Bay Bridge in 1952.

Because of the geography of the barrier island, investors knew that a railroad was the best way to transport vacationers to Ocean City. Starting in 1936, there were several attempts to provide state financial backing to construct a train route, but none was successful. Then, in 1876, Stephen Taber granted a right-of-way through his property to the Wicomico & Pocomoke Railroad. This transaction would connect Berlin, by rail, to the Sinepuxent Bay and what was to become the Ocean City beach. Once there was a way to get visitors to Ocean City more easily, early settlers and other interested parties saw the opportunity to house these visitors during their stay.

Hotels in Ocean City evolved from small modest one-story wooden structures which housed the earliest settlers, fishermen, hunters, and workers, into grand multi-story edifices reaching to the brilliant azure sky. Envisioning the promise of luring tourists, the barrier island began to provide basic lodging for weekend tourists at the end of the 19th century. These facilities were most often called inns, cottages, or rooming houses. By the second decade of the 20th century, these early hotels had added restaurants and entertainment venues designed to entice the city-weary to healthy relaxation by the sea.

The Blue Top Cottages, across the Herring Creek Bridge, are some of the few early cottages still standing. I include only a portion of the hotels in this chapter.[48] I chose these hotels because either we have stayed there or because these spaces enjoy historic significance.

From the beginning of human occupation, the land bordered by the Atlantic Ocean on the east and what is now Berlin to the west was settled by Native American peoples. The nations of the Assateague and the Pocomoke tribes signed a peace treaty in 1722 with Governor Charles Calvert, which essentially prescribed how the native Americans were to interact with the first landowners and how the individual members of each tribe could get permission for crabbing and hunting. This treaty followed one in 1662 with the Assateague and Nanticoke nations, which resulted in the granting of five reservation parcels of lands along the Pocomoke on the Eastern Shore for their peoples, and prescribed the payment of "six match coats" to the Emperor of that nation for a parcel of land by Europeans. Several other treaties by the end of the 17th century resulted in tribes moving north, possibly to escape from further encroachment by the white man. When the first Europeans arrived, the land was used as a grazing ground for wild boar and horses. Soon others discovered that this small piece of Atlantic paradise could be so much more.

Long before the fitness craze of the 1960 and 70s the seaside was touted as the answer to leaving behind the smokestacks and noise of the city. In a letter to *The Baltimore Sun* on August 27, 1869, we read:

> A new watering place for our sunbathing population is about to be established upon the Sinepuxent

Sea Shore and Atlantic Hotels

Bay, near this place. The matter is already in the hands of responsible, energetic parties.[49]

When the baby boomers look out from their 35th floor condominiums on 125th Street, many acknowledge that, in their youth, they didn't venture much beyond 15th Street. From the post-World War II years, when Ocean City was just getting its footing, the resort saw a tremendous investment in lodging houses, apartments, and small to mid-sized hotels which could house the vacationers.

When Isaac Coffin built the first beach cottage, the Rhode Island Inn in 1869, the hospitality industry for the barrier island was born. Ocean City's until that time was a barren barrier island on which cattle and livestock grazed at will. It was a far cry from a place that millions love to visit and about 7,000 make a year-round home.

The practice of opening up small hotels or inns began in

the mid-19th century. At that time most of the visitors were fishermen who only required modest lodging to rest the night. Early photographs from the late 19th century depict modest structures, some occupied by new residents and others made available for visitors to the barrier island.

Bill Gibbs, owner of the Dough Roller restaurants and the Breakers Hotel, tells me that his parents rented out his and his brother's bedrooms during the summer to vacationers. "We slept on the front porch," Bill remembers with a chuckle.

Rooming houses like Isaac Coffin's Rhode Island Inn built in 1869 dotted the beach landscape. There were not enough of these primitive structures to recognize the barrier island as a resort, but, in some way, they were forerunners of what Ocean City has become. They represented the hope that someday Ocean City would be able to attract sun-seekers from across the mid-Atlantic. These basic inns would be followed by one- or two-story small hotels along Atlantic and Baltimore Avenues and beachfront cottages. Some of the hotels were constructed in brick, but most were wood-shingled.

Growth spurred the desire to capture the vacation dollars of Marylanders by the largest, the latest, and the greatest hotels that $12 a week could buy. That was the advertised price of a room at the Atlantic Hotel in 1880 when yearly salaries in the country averaged $545.

The Atlantic Hotel

The *grande dame* of the fledgling hotel industry was the 400-room Atlantic Hotel, which opened for business on July 4, 1875. Its construction had been financed through stock sales in the Atlantic Hotel Company, and a year later Stephen

Taber sold to the fledgling government of the island 50 acres for the site of a town. Private owners were able to purchase a 25x142-foot lot from the Atlantic Hotel Company for $25.

Gordon Katz describes the land deal as follows:

> The exact terms of the deal are unknown. One report states that the company paid Taber $20,000 for the property. Other reports suggest that Taber agreed to deed the parcel contingent on the company first erecting a hotel on the site…As part of the deal, Taber also agreed to grant the Wicomico & Pocomoke Railroad a right of way across his farm at Hammock Point, paving the way for the completion of the essential rail connection from Berlin to the bay and then across it to the hotel on the beach…[50]

Because the hotel was one of the earliest full-service lodgings in the area, it housed many of the first meetings of po-

The New Atlantic Hotel with 1920 Bathers

tential developers for the new resort. As described in a later chapter, the Atlantic also served as the first worship space for the St. Mary Star of the Sea and St. Paul's by-the-Sea church communities.

Dr. Charles Purnell owned the Atlantic between 1923 and 1925. It burned down on New Year's Eve, 1925, in a fire that demolished many downtown properties. The Atlantic was rebuilt and has stayed in the Purnell family until today. Dr. Purnell was a grandson of Isaac Coffin, owner of the Rhode Island Inn. According to Bill Purnell,[51] when the family rebuilt the hotel in 1926, they

> ...built the south wing and the middle section after laying a new foundation and the iron work... and, in 1930 erected the north section to make the hotel shaped like an h...my grandfather was the owner and my father was the manager.[52]

Besides being attracted to the rich tradition of the Atlantic, "people used to come and stay ...one or two weeks...some stayed all summer with a trunk in tow because of the hotel's kitchen," current owner Bill Purnell recalls. "Not only did we have good food, we had plenty of it," Bill recounts.[53]

Guests would come down on the train, which at first ran right down to the Atlantic, with trunks for a long stay. The station was located on the east side of Baltimore Avenue between Somerset and Wicomico Streets behind the hotel. It was replaced in 1903 by a new facility when the railroad tracks were relocated from Baltimore to Philadelphia Avenue.

Porters from the hotel would go down to the train and later the bus station with wagons, pick up the luggage of guests and drop the bags off at the Atlantic and other hotels as far north as the Commander, 14th Street and the Boardwalk before the bridge was moved in 1933 after the Big Hurricane.

Dress codes have changed remarkably since Bill Purnell was young. "When I was a boy, to go down on the boardwalk... my father would be dressed in a sports coat, my mother a dress. If I had shorts on, I'd wear a sport coat and a summer shirt ..."[54] he remembers.

In a postcard of the original hotel dated about 1920, the postcard writer says:

> You'd meet a girl there, then get together with her again that afternoon on the beach. Then, in the evening, it was back to the Plim or the Atlantic for more dancing. At the Atlantic you had to pay 10 cents a dance to glide around the dark floor

Back view of The Atlantic Hotel
Photo by Ellen Marshall

lighted only by reflections from a big, turning ball, suspended from the ceiling and surfaced with hundreds of tiny mirrors. (Author unknown)[55]

Bill Purnell speaks of how the hotel was updated in 1926:

> They had enough money to build a steel foundation and the iron work...also they built it back like you see now, they built the south wall and the middle section in 1926 and in 1930 they did the north section. This was before I was born and my grandfather was the owner and my father the manager.[56]

The current footprint of the Atlantic Hotel has not changed. Its lobby is accessed through the Baltimore Avenue entrance off the parking lot, and hence no longer has a striking boardwalk presence. Visitors must look closely between boardwalk attractions to find its sign. Otherwise, many do not know it is an historic property of such renown.

Bill Purnell updated the lobby in 2013 and is proud to show off the new look. He recalls that the Atlantic boasted of its excellent kitchen where guests enjoyed three meals every day. Hotel restaurants were the only option for beachgoers before WWII. The Atlantic hired Paul Jones from South Carolina as its chef about 58 years ago. Chef Paul knew what the guests wanted and the hotel was able to host many important meetings during its early history. For example, the Democratic Women of Worcester County met at the Atlantic regularly since their founding in 1993. Spiro Agnew and his wife were frequent guests. Senator John F. Kennedy came to a dinner when he was campaigning for president, and took walks on the boardwalk outside the hotel. Mr. Purnell recalled his mother observing that "all the women swooned over the handsome Kennedy."[57] President Richard Nixon was a guest of the Atlantic.

Third-generation family owners like the Purnells continue the tradition of Ocean City hospitality at these downtown hotels. It is this dedication to customers and counting upon the word-of-mouth advertising of good service that built their businesses. The Atlantic is just one of the hotels in the original Ocean City which pride themselves on serving as summer homes to vacationers.

George Hurley, former Ocean City Council member and renowned local historian, spoke about the dedication of the early hotel owners to hard work and, occasionally, a savvy business sense. That combination kept the business in family hands during the ups and downs of the vacation real estate market. It would be folly to write a history of the growing hospitality industry and downplay the imprint these pioneers had upon the growth of the beach town as it became a thriving resort community.

Mr. Hurley researched the financial records of Ocean City. He found that when the Atlantic Hotel Company was founded, it was worth $25,000 and is now worth $8.9 billion.

Approximately 800 to 1,000 people lived in Ocean City during the 1930s and 1940s. Less than 50 of them became rich due to real estate investment, according to George Hurley:

> This is because most of the early residents were working class people – the fishermen, the store owners, the small hotel owners and worked for the service industry. Only a few had the capital and the ability to turn their modest investments into a real estate empire. Even fewer were able to survive the ups and downs of the resort's growing pains

before the building of the Chesapeake Bay Bridge.

Mid-20th century investors were able to purchase lots for $1.50 on the east side of Coastal Highway and $1.00 per lot for the west side after the city limits were expanded. Some of the lots sold to developers for $200,000 after the Bay Bridge was built.[58]

Much of the early history of Ocean City is entwined with the families who bought original lots from the Atlantic Hotel land transfer. Most of those families, like the Shreves, turned their early investment of $25 each for one of 108 lots into lucrative properties. They saw the potential of what the lots could become, temporary housing for vacationers. These early families erected hotels and small rooming houses. A dwindling number of these historic hotels still exist today. Today, remaining historic hotels are worth tens of millions of dollars and form much of the character of this Atlantic paradise.

The Summer Rental Experience - Mid 20th Century

To returning families to Ocean City like mine, the decision of where to rent their own slice of paradise for a few days, a week, or all summer was easy. That choice rested upon which part of Ocean City you either patronized with your family or where one felt most comfortable staying. Either you preferred the peace and quiet of the newer condos which can rise 30+ stories into the sky, or the busier downtown section near the wider beach and the boardwalk. My family loves to ride the waves and fall asleep hearing the pounding of the surf on the wide beaches. So we stay below 15th, usually between 5th and 9th and the boards.

Windows with screens invite into our apartment the wonderful ocean and bay breezes and the popular melodies of a guitar player. What could be better than that? Those family-owned older buildings, which have the tenacity to hold on against the onslaught of national hotel chains, make up for the modern amenities they might lack. They do that first by their lovely front porches. There I can continue my book, watch the boardwalk crowd, or just chat with new-found friends. As the Cheers theme goes, "everyone knows your name". So rich, so comforting, and so innocent and perhaps fleeting. I will enjoy these as long as I can. AHHHH!

Part of my comfort derives from the knowledge that many of the places we stay are owned and managed by women, as they always have in Ocean City. However, the economics of maintaining a wooden or siding structure against the wear and tear of the ocean environment is a challenge to their future. Current family owners face many of the same hurdles as the early "Ladies."

The Ladies Resort

Then, as now, one of the distinguishing features of many Ocean City hotels built at the end of the 19th and beginning of the 20th centuries is that they were owned and operated by women. In a 1926 advertising guide, 30 of the 32 hotels listed were owned by early female pioneers.[59]

Ocean City is so proud of these early hotel owners that it sponsors a permanent exhibit about them, *The Petticoat Regime of 1890-1926*, at City Hall, 301 Baltimore Avenue. In an era when men were often the businessmen and family heads, Ocean City stands out for its support of women hotel pioneers. Sometimes, the hotels started out of the necessity to earn extra income from rentals. But, whatever the motivation, women had the business savvy to operate these homes away from home for decades.

On June 2, 1884, Ella Dennis bought one of the original lots, Lot 81, of the Atlantic Hotel Company from a firm Robertson & Dixon and operated the Dennis Hotel. Josephine Hastings (The Shoreham), Rosalie Shreve (The Plimhimmon), Ethel Kelley (the Royalton), Elizabeth Hearne (the Belmont) , Minnie Jackson (the Shoreham), Minnie Mae Lynch (the Commander) and Mary B. Quillen (the Lankford) joined her among that prestigious group of foresighted women. 20th century female hotel owners, like Margaret Lambros (Lambros-Hampton House) and Marion Virginia Nichols Cropper (The Parker House) follow in the tradition of these early entrepreneurs.

In 1919 Susan Medora Dickerson Mason purchased the future site of the Mount Pleasant Hotel for $10,000. The lot was on the north side of Talbot Street. The hotel was eventually operated by several other owners and began its life as the Isle of Wight Cottage owned by Anna and Lemuel Showell. The Showells were experiencing financial difficulties on the three loans in 1897 which resulted in a foreclosure auction of all their Talbot Street properties. William Showell, who also ran one of the earliest bathhouses on the boardwalk, was a vestryman at St. Paul's Episcopal in Berlin.

Mrs. Mason retired from the hospitality business in 1933 when she was 71 years of age. Anna Showell deeded all of her remaining property assets to her daughter Nadine in 1908. Nadine operated the Hotel Sea Crest until her death in 1959. The Mount Pleasant itself was completely demolished by fire in 1970.

The Belmont Hotel

Another distinguished and fiery hotel entrepreneur was Elizabeth Harper Herne.

Elizabeth Harper Hearne and her husband, Dr. Thomas Hearne, moved to Ocean City from Bishopville in 1896. Their home became a haven for free-loading family and friends. Elizabeth decided to put a stop to her hosting of "unpaying guests" by renaming her home the Belmont Hotel in 1905 and posting room rates. It was located near North Division Street and the Boardwalk.

The Belmont was located on the Ocean block of Dorchester Street. It was renamed the Belmont-Hearne Hotel and operated by family members before it was torn down in 2004.

The Shoreham

An historic hotel continuing in operation, the Shoreham, was built by Josephine Richardson Hastings. Mrs. Hastings "was one of the most successful property owners in Ocean City."[60] Mrs. Hastings owned several other small hotels as well. When she built the Shoreham, she made certain that the 40 rooms had an accompanying bath. She also took advantage of advertising to her prospective market in one of the foremost daily newspapers. This advertisement placed in *The Baltimore Sun* on April 12, 1923 shows that she emphasized its location:

> THE SHOREHAM: Opens April 15, 1923. Ocean City's most up-to-date hotel. Just completed. New throughout. Private baths and running water. Directly on the Boardwalk. Mrs. Kendall C. Hastings, Ownership Management.[61]

The Shoreham is at the south corner of Boardwalk and 4th Street. Gordon Katz describes it as "the oldest hotel building in continuous service in Ocean City today."[62] Minnie Jackson bought the lot in 1892. She was a wealthy Baltimorean who bought two more adjoining lots in 1896 and built a cottage. One of her long-term tenants, Duane and Matilda Fox, threw parties every season for their friends vacationing at the Ocean.

Mrs. Jackson sold the property in 1913 and ownership was eventually transferred to Josephine Hastings. She expanded the footprint in 1922 to forty bedrooms and sixteen bathrooms. At that time, the name changed from the Hastings to the Shoreham. In 1926, the hotel was bought by Dr. Horace O. and Amanda Ayres Cropper. Raymond Shockley is the current owner.

We stayed at the Shoreham during Sunfest weekend, September 30-October 2, 2021. Knowing it was an historic hotel with no frills, we expected the smaller mid-1960s decorated rooms. Compared to what neighboring hotels on the boardwalk were charging for this popular weekend, the Shoreham was a bargain. It is right in the heart of downtown Ocean City and on the boardwalk.

Diane at the front desk was especially helpful and friendly. She filled me in on the ownership history and several great new restaurants to try. That's just what I expect from the smaller hotels who hire knowledgeable longtime residents to greet the guests.

Vacationers who only need a place close to the surf and boardwalk at a competitive price enjoy the Shoreham. The hotel has no elevators. During the season, expect noise from Shenanigan's restaurant on the ground level, when the music begins and the Guinness flows.

The Shoreham is rumored to be haunted by three ghosts.⁶³ The first ghost was a writer who committed suicide in the 1930s. In the late 1970s, the Shoreham had a bar in the basement. There the second ghost was killed by a Navy Seal. Betsey, who haunts Seasonal Room #6, jumped from a window in 1983.

The Lankford Hotel

The Lankford is a postcard-perfect place to stay when we want a quiet, relaxing few days. Their literature reflects their family-oriented values. Sally and Mary David Rutka⁶⁴ are third-generation caretakers of this 1924 hotel built by their great-great aunt, Mary B. Quillen. Mrs. Quillen transferred ownership to her niece, Betty Frame in 1964. It sits on the boardwalk between 8th and 9th Streets and is distinctive because of its three-story columns. The Lankford, with its 52 rooms, apartments and efficiencies currently has its hotel on 8th Street and the Boardwalk with apartments jutting out of the back towards Baltimore Avenue and others across 8th Street off the boardwalk.

Like other historical hotels, the Lankford shares the distinction of retaining family ownership. Many seasonal beach-goers appreciate that they are staying with a family and, in a sense, staying with friends. Of course, that is part of its charm. After all, how many of us know the Marriott family? The Travel Channel's "Hotel Impossible" crew spent 4 days there with a goal of updating the facility so it could be more competitive with other independent ocean front properties. Sally Rutka-Karst believes "...what it is we need to do something different. My mom was raised in the hotel. I was raised

Four-year-old Justin playing with Thomas Train Set in Lankford Lobby in 2019. Photo by Eugene Marshall

in the hotel. I guess it's time for change..."[65]

By Ocean City terms, the Lankford is an old-school operation because the family still runs it, not a property management company. They don't compete with brand-name hotel franchises, but instead are up against other small mom-and-pop hotels, some of which offer amenities that the Lankford doesn't have, like a swimming pool or an elevator.[66]

The Lankford is cushioned between a privately owned cottage, the Paradise Plaza, and the Majestic Hotel, another landmark property still in operation. Like most of the historic hotels, their dining rooms were a big draw. In 1956 a vacationer could buy a full-course meal in the Lankford's restaurant for $2.

Rooms are furnished simply, with one or two beds and a

dresser – mid 20th-century décor – with a refrigerator and window air conditioners. It is almost like staying in your grandmother's post-WWII home.

The Lankford has a large open lobby area and two wonderful front porches with rockers for people - watching or reading.

Two years ago, our grandsons were delighted that the lobby had a Thomas wooden train set for young visitors to enjoy. One of the long-time employees set up the train set, which he had originally bought for his sons.

In 2020, the Ocean City newspapers reported that the Lankford had been sold and that a new facility was to be erected on its site. That news was premature. The owners decided to wait another 5 years to sell, according to Mary.

In a recent interview with Mary David Rutka, who now operates the hotel for her family, she describes how the Lankford sees its marketing niche as the families who return each summer to continually make new memories. Those customers value the small family-friendly atmosphere, complete with that Thomas train track layout in the lobby. They wish to give their children the happy childhood Ocean City experiences that they vividly and fondly recall.

Mary sums it up:

> Our return customers are families and middle-aged and retired adults. We don't really advertise in the newspapers and trade magazines because we know this market. We love the families and they enjoy the Lankford for what is does offer. They know we do not have all the amenities of the newer hotels... 50 rooms versus 100 plus, restaurant, pool, etc.[67]

What are the challenges of operating a 95+ year-old facility? "The cost of upkeep when the facility is on the ocean. The ups and downs of the international student visas issued, because the hotel depends on that employment market in high season. Not having the resources to invest in seamless internet access and modern technological booking resources," Mary David responds.

The Lankford retains so much of the qualities of the downtown Ocean City hotels I stayed in as a child and teenager. We could open the screened window and immediately take in the aroma like none other. The salt and the sea smells hitched a ride upon the crisp ocean air to tell us we were in a summer place, a playground at the Ocean's edge. The older mid-20th-century furniture bore the scent of tens of thousands of families who called OC their temporary home. Dinner cooking on the old stove was unlike any food smell at home. Thrasher's French fries cooking, and onions being sautéed for steak subs, found our summer noses. Ah, we are here.

One returning family, the Burns/Heckler/Wroten/Caperna clan, have been vacationing at the Lankford for 18 years.

The Majestic Hotel and Apartments

One of the distinctive hotels, known for its picturesque front porch with rocking chairs, is the Majestic. When my family was young, we walked past it on the way to the 9th Street eateries and arcade. Many visitors rented their apartments, maybe for the entire summer season. To us, those season renters must have been rich, although by 1990 standards it was a bargain. Its history begins with an entrepreneur, Mrs. Rounds.

The Majestic Hotel
Photo by Eugene Marshall

Mrs. Rounds' experience in the hospitality business began when she took over ownership of the Avondale on Baltimore and Talbot. A visiting child's death falling from the Avondale balcony convinced the owner to give it up. In fact, they traded homes with the Rounds.

The Majestic was one of the Ocean City hotels which began operating as a long-term rental residence. The apartments were available to families as three-month rentals during the prime summer months of June, July, and August. This ensured funding to the Majestic's owners, while they were able to keep up the investments needed to maintain their beachfront properties. Although ownership was not transferred to the summer renters, this arrangement may have laid the foundation for joint-ownership in other soon-to-be-built condominiums in Ocean City during the building boom of the 1960s.

The Commander Hotel
Photo courtesy of John Lynch

One of the attractive features of the Majestic is its large, covered porch on the boardwalk, from which its patrons can rock and survey the boardwalk and beach crowds. This amenity continues to be a big drawing card for those used to watching the summer foot traffic from an East Baltimore marble stoop – and it's a lot cooler. Just as these part-time residents watch the boardwalk crowd, the boardwalk crowd returns the compliment and watches them rocking on the cooler summer evenings. A glimpse into the past 100 years is part of the summer experiences of Ocean City.

Priscilla Grasmick-Stone recalls how her mother, Marie Swintech Knop, enjoyed her July stays in a Majestic apartment facing the Atlantic Ocean:

> Mom stayed at the Majestic because the price was right. She loved the beach and loved going

to Ocean City each summer. Mom was a coupon shopper who could stretch a dollar at the Ocean and on her other trips by using coupons and other deal- saving strategies.[68]

The Commander Hotel

Minnie Mae Lynch, with her son John B. and daughter-in-law Ruth Jones Lynch, built the Commander at the northernmost point of Ocean City, 14th Street and the Boardwalk, in 1930. The Lynch family traces its roots as an 18th-century lower Shore family, in Berlin and Ocean City.

Earlier, John B. Lynch went into business with the Kelleys to build and operate the Royalton on 11th and the Ship's Café on the Bay and 14th. When John decided to operate his own hotel, according to his son John,[69] he pulled out his stocks, purchased the land, and built a hotel with over 100 rooms and a dining room that could serve 400.

Like many of Ocean City hotel owners, the Lynches took a huge gamble that the resort would flourish, and they would become wealthy. Wealth did come for some early families, but most of the early hotel owners earned a more modest income. The fact that the Commander stands today is a testament to the family visions and gritty determination that kept the hotels afloat even in leaner times.

Thomas D. Winbrow writes:

> During the summers of 1959 and 1960 I was employed by Mr. and Mrs. John B. Lynch, owners of The Commander Hotel located at 14th Street and the Boardwalk. The work I did for them during those two summers has provided me with won-

derful memories of "Old Ocean City". The job I had was Assistant to the Storekeeper for the Commander kitchen. The Storekeeper was William H. Parker, a retired Coast Guardsman known to all as "Bud". Bud was a tough old bird that ran a tight ship. Together we were responsible for supplying the kitchen staff with everything needed to provide meals for the hotel dining room.[70]

The Commander is one of the hotels which has the capital to continually modernize. In a recent stay, my husband and I were not only comfortable, but had Wi-Fi access. Their lobby is attractive, with a painting of Zippy Lewis prominently displayed. Rooms allow enough space for a long weekend stay.

The Lambros-Hampton House

I can still recall Mrs. Margaret Lambros, owner of this two-building apartment complex on the boardwalk between 4th and 5th Streets, ringing in the rental receipts. She gave out the apartment keys from her old clangy register in the first-floor boardwalk sundries store bearing her name. Mrs. Lambros was a shrewd businesswoman who knew her patrons and advertised regularly in the Baltimore newspapers. Her summer residence was in an apartment of Hampton House pictured below.

The Lambros-Hampton House
Photo by Ellen Marshall

Margaret Lambros bought the business and it stayed in family hands until 2013. Her son Gus took over the business's summer management duties when his mother could no longer. Gus and his sister sold the variety store space to Sunsations, but continued renting units of Lambros and Hampton House.

Over the years, Mr. Lambros[71] maintained the historic character of the lodgings in an effort to keep the Victorian look that reflected mid-Atlantic resort housing of the late 19th and early 20th century. That old Ocean City charm is what drew my family to rent August week vacations from the Lambros family for over 10 years. I would call Gus each spring to pick out my week, he would check his calendar while I waited, and the deal would be done. After a few visits, Gus and I would greet each other with a hug and kiss when I entered his 1st floor Hampton House office to check-in, and he would remark on how much the kids had grown since last summer. During the week Gus would check to see how we were enjoying our stay. I couldn't have had that conversation with the owner of the Waldorf Astoria.

Gus recalls a time during which condominium developers challenged zoning laws which barred buildings taller than four stories along the boardwalk within the original downtown limits. Unfortunately for us, Gus sold the Lambros Apartments and Hampton House in 2013. The Lambros was taken down. The new owner, who owns most of the Sunsations stores in Ocean City, built a restaurant and store on its former site.

The Parker House

Marion Cropper married her husband and lived with parents of a friend of hers, Mr. and Mrs. Charles Parker, Sr., in The Parker House while her husband served in WWII. The Parker family's presence in Worcester County reaches back to a century before, when they were landowners, land surveyors, farmers, and fishermen. Henry T. Parker bought original lot 127, owned by Elijah Carey, in an auction on August 28, 1897. That lot was the site of The Parker House.

In 1831 a storm brought severe damage to farmland at North Beach, about 10 miles south of the present location of Ocean City. Among those affected were Thomas and Col. Charles Parker who "lost 22 head of cattle"[72] due to the rise of the tide during the storm.

Gertrude Purnell Parker, "Miss Gertie",[73] operated their guest house with her husband and was noted as a "Pioneer Woman" in the centennial book of St. Paul's by-the Sea Episcopal Church. The authors wrote:

> ..."Miss Gertie" was a quiet pleasant lady as well as a "quiet giver." She had a special place in her heart for the young people and the Sunday School. She never wanted it known that funds for Christmas and Easter treats and other expenses were her gift. She strongly believed that this was the true way of giving...[74]

The Parker House, one of the early 20th century rooming houses, provided shelter for early Ocean City residents. The Croppers lived in a basement apartment in this Talbot Street rooming house until they built their own house in 1946.

According to Mrs. Cropper:

> I had a very close friend who came to Ocean City with her family... and then married into the family

The Plimhimmon on the Boardwalk at 1st Street
www.plimplazaoc.com

of the Charles Parker, Sr, a very prominent family. That friend was married to Charles Parker, Jr, who was called Pinky.

This is when I became active at St. Paul's By-the-Sea, as a Ladies' Guild member, a very industrious group. In late November each year the Guild sponsored an early Christmas craft bazaar and luncheon that was very popular. Among the crafts sold were crewel pillows and aprons that many residents and visitors bought each year for Christmas presents.[75]

The Plimhimmon

Rosalie Tilghman Shreve, the founder of this historic hotel on the boardwalk, moved to Ocean City in 1890 to open a summertime boarding house. The Ocean City Life-Saving Station Museum site describes the hotel's early history:

> It was so successful that, in 1894, at the age of 50, she ventures into a new business. She purchases two ocean front lots...and builds the Plimhimmon with its 48 rooms that could accommodate ninety people...The interior was (sic) quite plush with modern electricity and sanitary plumbing...
>
> was also famous for the quality and quantity of its food. For breakfast alone, a guest had his choice of any kind of hot or cold cereal, eggs made to order, kidney stew, lamb chops, bacon, toast, jam, fresh melon, coffee, tea and a wide variety of juices.[76]

The Plimhimmon took its name after the Shreve family estate, "Plynlimon," in Wales. That estate stood on "the highest point of the Cambrian Mountains."[77] Rosalie was the daughter of a very famous Marylander, General Tench Tilghman, and the Adjutant General of the State of Maryland. She was widowed at the age of 19 and had to support two children. Running a hotel proved to be a profitable way to do just that.

Dona Ang Yates recalls a time in the 1940s when the Shreve family was considering the sale of the hotel. Dona recounts with a twinkle and chuckle:

> In 1941 or 1942, my father was approached and the person offered to sell him the Plimhimmon Hotel for $600. My father said "no" because he thought he'd never get his investment back. After all, that was during WWII and before the Chesapeake Bay Bridge was built...[78]

On November 21, 1962, a fire broke out in the hotel, and it was rebuilt. Eventually the name was changed to the Plim

Plaza, and it still stands today. Its restaurant, the Paul Revere Smorgasbord was one of the must-go places for a summer vacation meal in the 1970s and 1980s before other buffet restaurants were opened on Coastal Highway.

Harrison Hall

The hospitality business in Ocean City, much like in the time of the pioneers who founded the original hotels, soon became a family affair. As the resort grew, the founding families' successors began buying other properties and building hotels upon them. These foresighted businesspersons got on the ground floor of a business that would grow to house the 8,000,000 annual visitors coming to this Atlantic Ocean paradise. Establishments like Harrison Hall, the Royalton, the Atlantic, the Belmont, the Breakers, and Plimhimmon were managed and owned by members of the original families well into the 20th century.

Harrison Hall
Photo by Eugene Marshall

Harrison Hall, founded in 1951 by Lois Harrison, is now managed by the Harrison Group and is run by her sons, John and Hale. Harrison Hall, at 15th Street and the Boardwalk, was the northernmost property in the resort town at that time. The Harrison Group continued to buy properties and now owns and operates 10 hotels, including the Shoreham, and several restaurants. The sons talk about growing up in a hotel family on the Harrison Group's website:

> "We learned to be the first in town, to set the pace and be ahead of the competition from Mother. Our father taught us the value of hard work and being morally ethical. We still stick to those same values today." - Hale Harrison

> "Dad died when I was 12. We worked in the hotel as boys after school, on the weekends, in the summer, anytime really to help Mom. We did everything you could think of, from desk agents to groundskeepers. We even lived there in the summers. We both have always known that's what we wanted to be when we grew up. We wanted to own hotels." - John Harrison.[79]

The Breakers Hotel

The Breakers Hotel at the Boardwalk and 3rd Street is another visual landmark that is visible from the beach or boardwalk. Its imposing four stories hold the corner of a wide intersection that has taken on many lives during its 60 plus year history. The original structure was built beside the Hastings, the Miramar, and the Westchester in 1904. It is a commanding

Breakers Hotel reflected in shallow on beach
Photo courtesy of David Sites

structure whose motto was "eat well-sleep well and be served well" in a 1940s advertisement. In a postcard of that time, its clapboard façade is painted green with a covered porch and striped awning. The 1936 image below shows the hotel in what appears to be white paint.

Changing façades and building materials for these historic hotels provide some insight into the kinds of maintenance required before each summer season to maintain a hotel's marketability. Those visitors who cherish the traditional architecture and look of the late 19th and early 20th century beach communities are the primary target for rental business, and they are a distinct market from those who rent modern high-rise apartments above 100th Street, preferring the view from on high with more modern amenities. In fact, it was the need to be more competitive in this expanding beach destination market that convinced current owners Bill and Julie Gibbs to raze the original Victorian structure and rebuild a modern facility. The Gibbs bought the Breakers from Mrs. Timmons in October 1980.

At the time the Gibbs bought the Breakers, the maids lived in basement rooms. Julie Gibbs would "have none of that" and rehabbed one of the better apartments on the first floor for their use. It was some of these same maids years earlier who had thrown Gibbs out by his ears because he was "doing something they didn't appreciate, like dragging sand into the space they had just cleaned."[80]

Another memory of Mr. Gibbs was that the Breakers was one of the few boardwalk hotels which had an umbrella room inside. When it rained, all of the other umbrella guys would seek shelter at the Breakers, making Tom one of the most popular guys on the boardwalk at a young age. He revels in that memory.

Between the extension of the railroad and the construction of the Bay Bridge in 1952, the hotels and businesses in Ocean City did a fair amount of business. Many of the early hotel owners and operators of the most popular restaurants became wealthy. Others provided a good living for the owners and decent summer jobs for the staffs. However, when the first Chesapeake Bay Bridge span was opened on July 4, 1952, hotel and condominium development exploded exponentially.

The Dunes Hotel, the Hastings and the Dunes Manor

Mrs. Thelma C. Connor, a longtime hotelier in Ocean City, decided to build a new hotel as far up as 27th Street at age 74. Her husband had died, and she wanted to realize their dream of owning a full-service hotel. So, she invested in the Dunes Manor, a hotel still operating at 15th and Boardwalk and where one can still enjoy an afternoon tea. The hotel is distinguished from its neighbors by its Victorian era look which includes a large porch front.

Thelma Conner was the daughter of Willye Jones and George Connor. Willye came to Ocean City in the early 1900s and met and married George, owner of the Conner's Restaurant, a longtime destination for locals and visitors. In 1922, they sold the restaurant and built the Hastings Hotel. The family also owned Dunes Manor and the Sea Hawk and Park Place, between 3rd and 4th Street and the Boardwalk. Park Place is located where the original Hastings Hotel stood.

George Hurley learned during his summer career as a contractor that Ocean City's growth spurred many of the original hotel owners to bring in the national chains to manage their properties. Not only did that strategy attract the financial backing of banks which could finance renovations and upkeep of their properties, but it also gave them the advantage of professional staff training and the draw of a known chain for vacationers.

The Hotel Roosevelt

Not many of the historic hotels built in the Victorian seaside style were able to withstand natural disasters. Many were washed away when hurricane flooding toppled the structures. Others, like the Atlantic, the Plimhimmon, the Breakers, and the Roosevelt fell victim to fire.

On Jan. 15, 1967, Tony Russo married his wife, Trudy, and in 1968 they opened the Roosevelt Hotel on N. Division Street and the Boardwalk. In 1970, half of the Roosevelt burned down and was redeveloped into a miniature golf course. In 1972, the second half of the hotel was burned in a fire, and

The Hotel Roosevelt

they converted the remaining structure into the iconic Tony's Pizza, a must-visit during a week at the Ocean.

Tony started his career when he arrived in Baltimore with his mother and worked at an equally famous local Italian pizzeria, Squires, in Dundalk, Eastern Baltimore County. So, when the Roosevelt succumbed to the flames, Tony and Trudy thought of that experience and opened in that spot as Tony's Pizza.

Expansion of the City Limits and Motels

As Ocean City expanded north and west, so did the need for additional lodging space. It was in the 1960s that motels cropped up along Coastal Highway. The Santa Maria and the Stowaway were among the first to create what is known as "Motel Row."

The Condo Craze

Very few of these early pioneers envisioned that tiny little rooming houses would become motor hotels in the late 1950s, when automobile traffic became the preferred mode of travel to Ocean City. Fewer imagined that multi-story condominiums would create a much different landscape from 60th Street to the Delaware line.

As in its earliest days, economics and Mother Nature played a major role in the city's expansion. The major storm in 1962 created one of Ocean City's greatest challenges, but also one of the resort's greatest opportunities since the Chesapeake Bay Bridge opening 10 years prior. Before the storm, Ocean City's tax base was not sufficient to support the laying of sewer lines and power cables, beach replenishment and other infrastructure improvements needed for expanding the resort. Incremental annexation became plausible because of the storm of 1962.

Recovering from the damage involved requesting and receiving EPA money. This infusion of federal dollars provided the necessary money to dig and lay the sewer lines and expand the electricity cables for both the Bay and Ocean development, as well as replenish sand that the storm had washed away. After all, it is hard to build a beach community without a wide enough beach to sun upon. Once the infrastructure was in place, the developer floodgates opened wide.

Early families like the Harrisons and Showells had purchased property beyond 14th Street on the ocean, and up to the Delaware line on both the bay and ocean sides of the barrier island. If their gamble paid off, the families stood ready to become millionaires. Thanks to the storm of 1962, when federal money became available to build the infrastructure, construction began in earnest, improving property values. Digging began on what was to become Montego Bay and Ocean Pines.

George Hurley recalls taking a summer job in construction to support his family. When he was standing on the higher level girders of what was to become the Carousel Hotel at 101st Street, he noticed the frantic pace of excavation on the bayside. He talks about those investment opportunities opening up:

> I went to an estate auction, it must have been in 1973 or maybe 1974 , ... when the building boom collapsed...where a whole block of land was being auctioned off between 58th and 59th Street. I want-

Large new house in West Ocean City overlooking the bay
Photo by Eugene Marshall

ed to bid on a block of land so I could acquire an underwater lot, that was attached to it, in the inlet. You couldn't vote in Ocean City at that time unless you owned land...John Dale Showell bought the whole block of land for $300,000. Hale Harrison, who owns Harbor Watch, Westward Ho, Harrisons and twelve other properties, went up to him (I was standing next to him) and said," I will write you a check now for $100,000 for what you just bought. The Harrisons sold the land to a developer for condominiums...I am just giving an example of how, if you had capital, you could make a big profit. And the land that I wanted and thought would go for $200 sold for $2500. I turned to Mr. Williams, a city lawyer, and asked, "Why would anyone pay $2500 for a lot that was underwater?" And he said, "George, you can't have a liquor license in Ocean City unless you own land."[81]

Real estate investors really became interested in the Ocean City market after the Chesapeake Bay Bridge was built in 1962 and the land up to the Delaware line was annexed in 1965. Some of the investors were local. Other families from Maryland and Pennsylvania saw the opportunity to own a second home for vacations and the rental market. One infamous investor, Bobby Baker, drew many not-so-tame headlines in the 1960s and 70s.

Mr. Baker was an influential member of Lyndon B. Johnson's staff when he was in the Senate. He began his political career as a Congressional Page. When Bobby Baker was still working in Washington, he looked to Ocean City as a way to make money quickly. Due to his political connections, Baker was able to get Washington money to invest in Ocean City. This article from *OC Today* describes the opening of The Carousel:

> On the day of the Carousel's opening on July 22, 1962, then Vice-President Johnson and his wife, Lady Bird, arrived in a limousine, while 200 senators, congressmen, lobbyists and congressional staffers swilled champagne on the way down in seven chartered buses.
>
> The hotel also drew a great number of locals who were fascinated by its glitz, glamor, clientele and two bars. The Carousel was like nothing Ocean City had ever seen and it put the resort on the national map.

Baker's investments at a time when he was making only $20,000 as a Senate staffer resulted in legal scrutiny and eventually conviction on tax evasion, bribery and fraud. Yet, the expansion of building hotels and condominiums also opened ownership opportunities for many. It also changed the landscape of Ocean City forever.

While visiting Ocean City, either for a day or a week, we plan on eating at some of the resort's amazing restaurants. The following chapter describes several of those eateries for breakfast, lunch, dinner or happy hour.

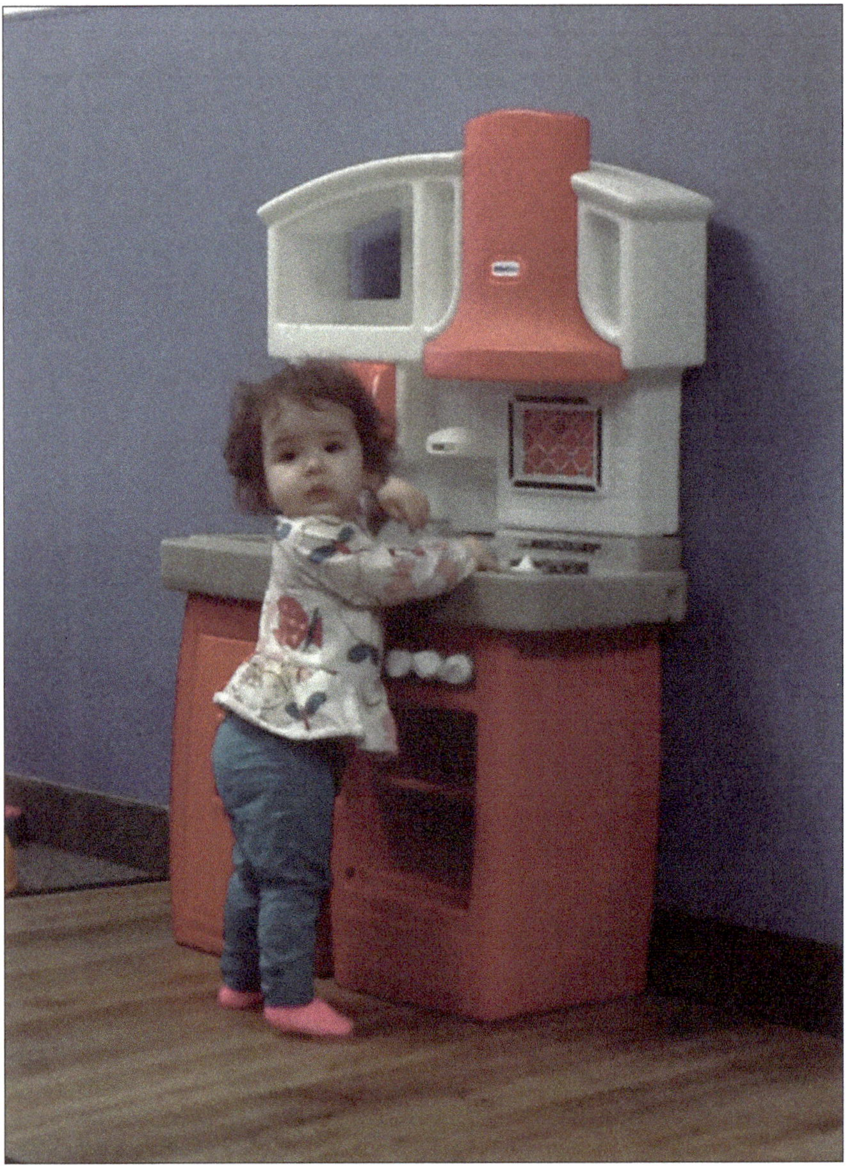

Where We Eat

"A thing of beauty is a joy forever: it's loveliness increases; it will never pass into nothingness."

John Keats

Vacation is a time when you throw away the diet, forget about cooking on the stove for a week, and eat, eat, eat. In Ocean City. what you eat is crabs, corn on the cob, crab cakes, crab omelets, French fries, and pizza. To top off a decadent meal, try the ice cream sundaes, shaved ice, and key lime pie. Ah, can't you taste summer now? Those of us who like to plan our "must-have" meals have our favorites where we return, visit after OC visit. Others make spontaneous decisions about eating venues, maybe based on the, *pssst*, did you see discount coupons in the *Vacation Guide*? Yes, advertising pays in Ocean City, Maryland.

Ocean City gives a visitor hundreds of eatery choices, 200 and growing,[82] according to the official Ocean City visitor's website. Each season it seems that more restaurants open. One fun activity this author enjoys is driving on Coastal

Thrasher's French Fries at 9th and Boardwalk
Photo by Eugene Marshall

Highway towards Delaware and seeing what new places have opened during the off-season. Is that one worth a try? Or perhaps we will just stick with our favorites....

Breakfast

Breakfast is the first real meal decision we must make. Although we likely checked in on Saturday or Sunday afternoon, that might be a meal that is very casual, like close-by pizza delivery. Sometimes the breakfast choice is made by the noses and eyes of early-morning bike riders. Where do they hide those fans that waft "eat me" aromas onto the boardwalk?

Often we make that meal decision based on who is or is not along. If the family unit includes toddlers, we are looking for family-friendly, full breakfast or pick-up donuts. Both extremes can be covered by Layton's, the restaurant where you can spot the long table where Ocean City notables dine every morning around 7:00 AM. Layton's Dip N' Donuts Family Restaurant on 16th and Philadelphia is famous for its daily specials written on the dry-erase board at the front. My mother always advised, "When travelling, go where the locals go."

Layton's

"We evolved basically from a basic donut shop, open 24 hours, to a full-blown menu,"[83] said Larry Layton. He, along with his wife Peggy, runs this popular restaurant where a family needs to time its arrival, or wait for a table.

In a beach town so much of a business's success depends on the relationship the owners have with their customers. In

Ocean City, where there are so many restaurants to choose from, Layton's has built its business model upon maintaining quality, giving people what they want – comfort food – and having a friendly and efficient wait staff. Oh, yes, and the wonderful smell of donuts as you walk through the front door.

The fact that a small business has stood the test of time is a tribute to the hard-working families like the Laytons who have dedicated their lives to growing their businesses and knowing their customers. "I have a great staff, they're friendly and they really bring a warm feeling to customers and that's what it's about,"[84] Larry says.

We can count on the old standbys like eggs and pancakes, or go out on a limb. Order the Eastern Shore Crabber, which consists of a home-made crab cake in a three-egg omelet with cheese. Oh my, can't you taste that Old Bay now? And, when we pay our bill, we will be tempted by the display of fresh-baked donuts in the nearby display case. If that is not enough to lure you, Robert (Larry) visits each table with donut samples for the kids of all ages.

Pam[85] explains why they are in the restaurant business in a recent interview:

> My husband started working at Layton's for his father when he was 14 years old. Originally we were a donut and coffee shop. Larry went to "Dunkin Donuts School" in the early '70s... Eventually the restaurant evolved into a restaurant... They purchased Layton's from Larry's dad and mom ... Larry loves the people, he's a very social person... and this has been our livelihood.[86]

When I asked what their business strategy is, Pam responded, "We keep plugging away, day after day, that is our strategy."[87]

Obviously, that business plan has worked. The Laytons celebrated the restaurant's 50th anniversary in 2018.

Soriano's

Soriano's is in the heart of downtown Ocean City, on Baltimore near Somerset. It is family-owned since 1982. Our family, like many return visitors, found this comfortable eatery with breakfast favorites in the 1990s.

Here, we can get the favorites – good omelets, pancakes and French toast – for a reasonable price. Their coffee is excellent, always hot and welcoming on a crisp morning. Spe-

Soriano's Facing Baltimore Avenue at Somerset
Photo by Eugene Marshall

cials, like homemade creamed chip beef or omelets, are popular choices.

When we visited in October 2021, I was able to catch-up with the owner, who recognized us. She explained that, in 2020, when COVID-19 caused a dip in visitors, the restaurant struggled. "Fortunately, we had a great year in 2021."[88]

Bayside Skillet and Fractured Prune

For a fancier breakfast we go to the Sunday morning favorite of vacationers and locals, Bayside Skillet. Delicious aromas of crab, pancakes a-frying, fresh fruit, and cheese greet the hungry as they exit their cars. Their specialties include crab omelets, crab, in-season fruit crepes, and brioche French toast. The wait staff don't seem to mind your lingering over a meal, even though the lines waiting at the front door may be long. And the coffee is superb!

And then there is Fractured Prune, a freshly made donut shop that kids of all ages love. Plain donuts await our topping preference at the time of an order. But then, all the flavors sound and taste great. I am salivating now as I write. The Prune is part of a chain, but the freshly topped donut choices seem to delude me into thinking they were baked especially for me. What a clever business decision!

Lunch, lunch, my kingdom for some lunch

No matter how much a family enjoys swimming, jumping the waves, and sunbathing, their stomachs tell them it is time for lunch. So, the designated picker-upper rises from his or her blanket and usually treks to a nearby boardwalk storefront restaurant. The nose usually rules in the choice of what to eat, and the nose has lots of choices if you are swimming in the Atlantic near downtown OC.

Tony's Pizza on the Boardwalk at Division Street offers – what else? – pizza, plus subs and sandwiches. If we don't want to take our carry-out down to the beach, Tony's also has a rooftop deck. From there we can look down at the people strolling the boardwalk. Tony's has been at that location since 1962.

If we just can't get enough of the French fries at **Thrasher's**, there are several locations close to where many are swimming and sunbathing. The original location is at the pier, but we can also stop at 2nd or 8th Street during the season (essentially Memorial Day through September). Thrasher's has been serving their delicious fries for 90 years.

Thrasher's website proclaims the reason for their popularity:

> Through five generations and eighty years, Thrasher's has changed hands only twice. Tradition rules and quality reigns supreme. There will be no deviation from original procedures or original recipes. Only experience and exquisite attention to detail have allowed Thrasher's to grow and flourish as few businesses have, nowhere will more emphases on quality be found. Nowhere will be a better fry be found - anywhere![89]

The storefront restaurant seems to have maintained the vision of its founder, J.T. Thrasher, since 1929. Only the Trimper's carousel is older!

The Dough Roller is another Ocean City eatery which keeps customers coming back year after year. Bill Gibbs, current owner of the Breakers Hotel and the Dough Roller restaurants (4 additional locations), opened the first location when he bought and renovated the Breakers in 1979. As a local teen in the 1960s, Bill rented beach umbrellas and chairs from under the porch of the Breakers. When it rained, the other guys who rented beach stuff would crowd into Bill's space. That location became the focal point for a family-friendly restaurant which offers pancakes, chicken and pizza.

The wonderful aroma of pit beef and onions fills the air at 2nd Street and draws people in. They stand in front of the Bull on the Beach, an Ocean City boardwalk eatery featuring falling-out-of-the-bread roast beef sandwiches. In case beef doesn't tempt you, how about a Reuben, a chicken or shrimp salad sandwich, or wings, or nachos?

Located on 2nd Street and the Boardwalk, the Bull opened its first outlet on May 28, 1980. If we don't feel like pit beef and a National Boh beer (not on the beach, though, since alcohol is not allowed), don't worry – the Bull will fill our gut. Owners Phil and Marie have figured it out.

The Chesapeake Bay, Land of Pleasant Living

The bounties of the sea have been one of the major defining pasttimes and industries of the Chesapeake Bay communities. For millenia, fresh fish, crabs, and oysters have kept watermen happily employed. From the moment one enters the Ocean City environs, this strong connection to the sea and its inhabitants is apparent.

First of all, when you travel via US 50 East and approach the village of Shantytown in West Ocean City, the first sight is of people enjoying sportfishing off the pier. Alongside the west bank of the Sinepuxent Bay, which flows into the Ocean, dozens of fishing boats line the harbor and dot the seascape. Then, as you turn into the town, your next visual is the white marlin sculpture and fountain. All are tributes to the Ocean City fishing tradition carried into the present.

As the White Marlin Capital of the World, Ocean City attracts many species of fish, not just Marlin. Fresh catch end up on the resort's dinner tables. During the busy summer season, fishermen catch sharks, bigeye and yellowfin tuna, sea bass, flounder, wahoo, and, notably, marlin.[90]

The Commander Hotel Dining Room Experience

Until the enactment of the Public Accommodations Act of 1964, restaurants in Ocean City were not required to serve African-Americans. In Ocean City segregation was part of the culture alongside hotel stays and dining. However, some of the most noteworthy persons in the hospitality industry were African- Americans.

James C. Wright, *maitre d'* of the dining room at the Commander on the Boardwalk and 14th Street, was one of those notables. Mr. Wright was hired by owner Minnie Mae Lynch in 1940. His son, Matthew, tells us about his dad in his book.

> Later, Mrs. Lynch handed control of hotel operations to her son Mr. John Lynch and the excellent food and service was extended as its trademark and established the Commander Hotel as a sought after refuge for relaxation, a cocktail and a delicious evening meal in the dining room. For my father and mother, the season began in late March to early April when all of his waiter staff assembled, at our

home on Fulton Avenue in Baltimore. People came from Virginia, Florida and all over, but if you were on my father's staff you left from his house by caravan on a given day to go to Ocean City. His dining rooms were always in immaculate order and his staffs were run like a fine-tuned engine. He was taught by his elders in the hotel trade and in turn he continued fine dining services throughout his career.

There was an art to the work you carved out in the hotel trade as being associated with you. For instance, when my father arrived on the dining room floor he always double-checked the reservations making sure that his best guests had his most seasoned staff. He would gather his staff prior to opening the dining room by making a smooching sound to give them assignments and last minute [sic] directions. He felt that major sounds and movements in the dining room were to come from the patrons' staff, he deemed to be invisible! As "maitre d' "he provided seating to his guest according to their stature and long patronage of the hotel. A good example of his artful efforts was that if a guest did not recognize good service and the tip was less than acceptable when they again requested an ocean-view, my father would seat them at the mirror rather than to give them a true ocean-view. No glass of water was to go beyond half full and each time a cocktail was about finished, the drink was immediately refreshed until the guest

The Commander Hotel Dining Room Staff
Photo courtesy of John Lynch

requested nothing else to drink. It was like clockwork from late March until mid-October.⁹¹

Mr. Wright was nicknamed Brown Sugar by the patrons of the hotel. And his son recalls that he was "Little Sugar."

Dinner's On

To a Marylander the smell of crabs steaming in vinegar, water, and Old Bay is a sure sign of summer. The Chesapeake Bay blue crab is synonymous with "the land of pleasant living," the Eastern Shore. So many of the Ocean City restaurant menus feature this selection on their dinner offerings.

To a genuine crab lover fresh cannot be beat. From the trap to the pot to the table to your mouth – heaven. When crabs are in season, heaven is just around the corner – *every* corner. Crabs come in early mornings from Eastern Shore crabbers, plucked squirming and fighting from Chesapeake Bay or the many rivers. These luscious crustaceans make a visit to Ocean City worth the drive.

Hooper's and the Angler Restaurant

The OC eater can find crabs on almost every block of Ocean Gateway. As soon as we approach the Ocean City bridge, yes the one which proclaims on a sign "3,073 miles to Sacramento," we can spot the Hooper's sign. Its structure, built in 1979, experienced a fire that spawned a complete makeover plus an entire block of development. Like many OC eateries, it remains family-owned. At **Hooper's**, one orders crabs by the dozen, and crab pretzels, and crab soup, and did I mention crabs? There may be other items on Hooper's menu, but you might get some weird looks if you aren't eating steamed crabs.

For hundreds, if not a thousand years, oysters also reigned supreme on the Eastern Shore of Maryland and Virginia. Relic hunters have discovered oyster shells discarded by Native Americans piled high along the shores in Crisfield, the Chesapeake Bay, and Hooper's Inlet. There are pen and ink sketches of the Eastern Shore's first inhabitants feasting on oysters.

Along the bay front, where fishing boats and sightseeing boats anchor, we find the Angler Restaurant nestled between clapboard houses. The Angler is one of the eateries that advertises on the banner of biplanes which fly the shore lined with tens of thousands of bathers every day in summer -- talk about a captive audience. Their pitch? Free boat ride with purchase of an entrée. So families line up at 4:00 PM to order crabs, or crab cakes, or oysters, or one of a dozen other seafood choices.

The Angler opened in 1938. Their website tells of their beginnings:

> Around the turn of the 20th century, Charles Rollins Bunting, great-grandfather of the present Buntings, purchased the property where the Angler Restaurant now stands. At that time there was no dock, only marsh grass through which the first Buntings pulled their sail bateaux and rowboats to shore.[92]

The restaurant started with a small idea, selling homemade desserts in 1938, but blossomed into a full-service restaurant. The storm of 1933 wiped away the dock and the buildings. In 1945, the Buntings rebuilt a new dock and reopened as a joint restaurant and sportfishing operation.

The extra experience of the sightseeing boat ride, especially after dark, is the draw for many visitors to the Ocean resort. Naturally, seafood is the focus of menu. I recall one summer when much of my birth family and their spouses and children vacationed the same week in Ocean City. Our big meal was at the Angler, everyone loved their meals and we went on the boat ride. It was an amazing evening, capped off by the view of our hotels along the boardwalk from the boat.

Phillips

The Phillips family, who operate the Phillips Restaurant, is one of Ocean City's early pioneer families. Shirley Phillips will go down in OC history for her crab cakes, a highlight of the St. Paul's by-the-Sea Episcopal Church's fundraiser, "Antiques by the Sea." Phillips started over a century ago as a processing distributor located on Hooper's Island, shipping to Baltimore restaurants. Then the Phillips family opened the restaurant at 17th and Philadelphia.

Many families testify that they go to Phillips every year for their Hooper's Island crab cakes, stuffed flounder, or clam bucket for two. The more adventurous might opt for the dinner all-you-can-eat buffet. Phillips has other restaurants in Atlantic City and Baltimore-Washington Airport. These days, they ship crab cakes which were packed in the Philippines.

The Phillips family announced in December 2021 that their Ocean City restaurant will be sold.[93]

Harborside Bar & Grill

If you want a good meal, go to a place frequented by locals. Harborside in West Ocean City fits that bill. In season, we might have to wait for a while to be seated before we can dive into one of their excellent seafood dishes or sip their famous original Orange Crushes.

> Harborside owners Chris Wall and Lloyd Whitehead, along with their friend Jerry Wood and bartender Kelly Flynn, invented the Crush more than 20 years ago… in 1995" The recipe is pretty straightforward – orange juice, orange vodka, triple sec and lemon-lime soda – and it keeps customers coming. "It's a drink created in Maryland, by Marylanders, and by all accounts that's good enough for them."[94]

But then, if you are at Harborside for more than drinks, I suggest you move from the bar to a harborside table and order from a menu that features such local favorites as softshell crab. Did I forget to mention the view? Since the restaurant

The View from the Harborside Grille
Photo by Eugene Marshall

is nestled on a pier along a harbor, a diner can top off the meal watching a glorious sunset. This experience makes you remember why you travelled to Ocean City.

Taphouses

For an upscale pub menu and great beers on tap, we visit the Taphouses. Two are on the boardwalk, at 4th Street and at 9th in The Paradise Plaza Hotel. The 45th Street Taphouse is on bayside with a glorious view of sunset on the bay. Zev Sibony, owner, added a fourth location at 137th Street in the Bayside Plaza.

Whatever your choice of sandwich or entrée, remember to upgrade to their parmesan rosemary fries. We feel comfortable taking our young grandchildren to the 9th and 45th

Street venues because of the casual, family-friendly atmosphere. Many other families do the same.

On a recent visit to the 4th Street Taphouse, we were happy to see one of our favorite Taphouse bartenders, Woody. It is so refreshing to return to Taphouse and other Ocean City restaurants to be greeted with "Welcome back, so nice to see you again."

Jonah and The Whale

Ahoy, matey. If we want to eat in an all-you-can-eat seafood restaurant with pirate-ship décor, we drive to 26th Street. Jonah and The Whale Seafood Buffet has been in the Ocean City, MD area since 1976 and is modeled upon an authentic whaling tavern.

Jonah was one of the first venues in Ocean City offering an all-you-can-eat buffet bar that included crab legs. Vacationers seem to relish this valuable commodity since so many other buffet bars have opened since Jonah and the Whale. But, like any other eating experience, families like ours return to those eateries when they enjoy their first taste.

When our children were young, we made Jonah our big meal of the week. I can still remember cracking open many luscious crag legs, dipping them into the melted butter sauce, and *ahhhh*. Another feature on the buffet bar was a raw bar where you could sample fresh oysters, clams, and mussels. Compared to many raw bars at which we have dined, buffet prices at Jonah and the Whale were a bargain for families.

The rise in 2021 seafood prices resulted in the restaurant charging an extra fee of $50 for crab legs. It is not clear whether these costs will stabilize.

Jonah and the Whale
Photo by Eugene Marshall

Embers

Being on vacation at Ocean City is so much of a sensory experience. From the saltwater smell coming into the resort town, to the sounds of Trimper's Rides at the pier, to the glorious sunrises and sunsets, everything about Ocean City is otherness. That is one of the reasons we go on vacation, to vacate or leave what are our normal lives and venture for a while into another world. Maybe that is one of the reasons why buffets do well at the Ocean.

Sam and Irving Taustin decided that 9th Street and the Boardwalk was the perfect place for their restaurant in 1945. And, considering that 9th Street was very popular, with some stores and an arcade, their hunch turned out to be a valuable investment.

The Taustin brothers also took advantage of the growing popularity of billboards along Route 50 before entering the beach town. As a child I remember our driving past these bigger-than-life pictures, promising culinary delights. At that point in the trip, when we can almost smell the sea salt, our senses are already excited. "Look, Mommy, can we go there?'" could be heard coming from every other car. We could not wait.

"Sam's goal for the restaurant was to serve the best food and give the most attentive service to every customer who walked in the door, and that continues to be the mission of the family today,"[95] the Embers website tells readers.

Embers is also noted for its steaks and prime rib. How could a diner go wrong with surf and turf? Great business informed the decision to relocate to 23rd and Coastal Highway where the parking and space allowed for a growing customer base.

Higgins

Another popular destination that features crabs is Higgins on Coastal Highway. Like so many Ocean City businesses, it has been owned and operated by several generations of one family. Their menu includes hard and softshell crabs and a variety of fresh fish.

Higgins opened on 31st and Philadelphia Avenue in the 1970s. They opened a second location at 128th street, close to the high-rise condos.

Often the decision of where to eat out at Ocean City was informed by the advertising banners. They are pulled by biplanes crossing the seascape near the shore. Beachgoers, sit-

Angler Restaurant and Route 50 Bridge
Photo by Ellen Marshall

ting in their chairs, watch the planes and naturally read their messages. Of course we all did. It has become part of the OC experience that is people and sight-watching from the comfort of a beach chair. That sight plants the seed for a dinner or after-hours plan.

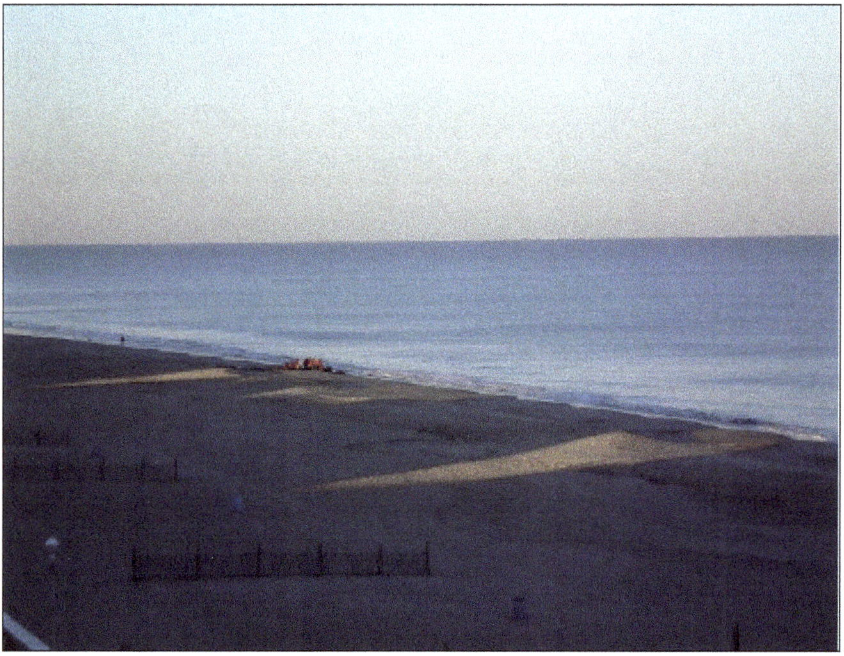

Where We Worship

Train whistles are the backdrop of life
The whooowhoo hangs behind other city sounds
It becomes an unacknowledged rhythm
Beating inside our hearts.

Ellen Knop Marshall

"Why do I have to go to church?" the kids would say. "I'm on vacation." Since Sunday is usually the second day of our beach week and our first chance to swim, no one wants to delay the fun by going to Mass. So when it comes to rousing our teenagers out of their salt-air slumber, I sometimes failed miserably. If I was successful, I was prepared for the flinging of good clothes here and there, the inevitable "Oh, Mom, do I hafta?," and a quick slide through the side door of Holy Savior Church on 17th and Philadelphia.

Something about being at the beach tempts us to lay aside the normal obligations – work, cooking, and, yes, even Sunday services. During the time before cell phones, laptops, and iPads, very few thought about being in touch with the office, let alone a church. Vacation is vacation, after all. You were down at the ocean to relax and enjoy children, friends, and grandchildren.

The normal vacation week begins on Saturday or Sunday in July or August. If families stayed in an apartment, there was a kitchen to prepare breakfast and other meals. Mom would often get a break from cooking one or two suppers during the week away. But what to do about church? The question resounds especially for Catholics, who knew Mass was an obligation. Could we stay away from church on the second day we were there, when the ocean was beckoning? Wouldn't God make allowances when He knew we were enjoying this beautiful beach He created? Didn't we get a "get out of hell" pass for one week a year?

Similar to many travel destinations, the churches played a major role in Ocean City's development. Members of those churches were also many of the founders and business people.

As the resort was growing in the popularity, church leaders of several denominations acquired the land to build places of worship in Ocean City.

Bishop Thomas A. Becker, of the diocese of Wilmington, Delaware paid the princely sum of $100 on May 25, 1878, for three lots, Nos. 55, 73, and 74.[96] There he built the first permanent Catholic church in the emergent town of Ocean City. The land stood on the southwest corner of Baltimore Avenue and Talbot Street. Worshippers gathered for Mass from 1877 until 1880 in a room in the John Myers Cottage, rented by John Tracy, the founding manager of the Atlantic Hotel. Construction was completed "by the end of August. Ocean City's first church was christened St. Mary Star of the Sea."[97]

This was a significant move because it was the first Church to be established on the barrier island. It is even more meaningful because there were no permanent residents of Ocean City in 1880.[98] Its first Catholic resident was Mr. William McHugh.

> During his stay in Ocean City, he owned a hotel in Snow Hill. Jesuit Fathers Chambers and Akers describe Mr. McHugh as "A native of Shelltown on the Pocomoke River, McHugh seems to have taken up residence here in 1898. Not much else is known, except that he...is buried in Baltimore." Mrs. Lenora Henry, the wife of Zadok P. Henry, was the first Catholic resident of Berlin.[99]

Each summer from 1868 to 1886, Wilmington Bishop Thomas A. Becker "spent his summer months at Ocean City. Once during the season all the priests of the Diocese joined the Bishop for an annual retreat."[100] Until the Ocean City Flyer arrived at the beginning of the 20th century, the Bishop appointed visiting priests to preside over the few attending Sunday Mass.

Bishop Becker realized that it would be difficult to attract priests to a ministry on the lower Eastern Shore. We read his words from his daybook of April 19, 1873, quoting from his report of January 12, 1873 to the Society for the Propagation of the Faith in Paris:

> ...all together he had at that time nine students studying for the priesthood in Baltimore, Rome and Louvain. There was a special need, he said, for priests able to speak German, that there were enough German-speaking people to make a separate congregation, and that he had spoken to the Jesuit Provincial for a priest...[101]

Bishop Becker "On September 4, 1874 made a strong plea in writing to the Provincial of the Maryland Benedictines Province:

> My dear and respected Fr. Provincial...but simply to assert what I know to be for the good of religion, especially in that sad territory called 'the Eastern Shore of Md.'...Therefore, finally, I demand as a right of the Church, that you forsake not the mission...[102]

The impetus to construct a church for Roman Catholics in Ocean City comes as much from the teachings of the Baltimore Catechism, Number I, which every Catholic memorized in question and response form.

For example: "Who is God? God is the Supreme Being who made all things..." "What is the Second Commandment? Keep holy the Lord's Day."[103] According to Catholic teaching of the time, it was a mortal sin not to attend Sunday Mass. If a local Church did not exist, Catholics travelling to the Ocean would have to go to Salisbury for Sunday Mass or risk damnation of their immortal souls. Getting to the town couldn't have been a cakewalk. Most vacationers came by train, crossing the Sinepuxent Bay into the resort. Salisbury lies about 25 miles north of Ocean City.

Michael Morgan writes:

> ...the railroad between Salisbury and Berlin had not yet been completed. Vacationers heading for the ocean had to travel over a dirt road to the west shore of Sinepuxent Bay, where they boarded a small boat and were ferried over to the barrier island."[104]

So, it made sense to locate a church closer to where vacationers were staying.

In a ten-page history written by a member of St. Mary's in 1954, we read that a "Mrs. Dennis, a woman with a keen memory... and the oldest living resident of Ocean City"[105] recalled details of the church's founding:

> As a young girl, Pairs Dennis remembers three buildings in Ocean City and one of them was the Catholic Church. It was a sparsely settled place with only five white families in Ocean City...This would tally with the account given by Mrs. Dennis that the Church was built in late 1876 or 1877. She tells us that the Church was a small chapel for as we know it was built for the purpose of accommodating the summer congregations of vacationist[sic].[106]

Archival sources are in conflict about the exact year of the opening of St. Mary's. A pamphlet celebrating the new pipe organ contains a brief history of the Church and recounts:

> In the remodeling of the church of Our Lady, Star of the Sea, an old board was removed and saved by one of the parishioners because it bore this legend: "John Stack, Builder, Baltimore, Md., March 8, 1882." This board furnishes us with definite proof that the Church was built under Bishop Thomas A. Becker, the first Bishop of Wilmington, just four years before he was succeeded by Bishop Alfred A. Curtis.[107]

When construction on the Church was complete, lot number 73 remained vacant. The Diocese of Wilmington sold the land to the Ocean City Volunteer Fire Company in 1927 for $10. The firehouse built on that site is still in operation.

Saint Mary Star of the Sea Church: 1900 to Present

The population of Ocean City grew as did the parishioners of St. Mary's. Bishop John J. Monaghan of the Wilmington Diocese enlarged the Church in 1907 and added a gothic tower. Within the tower he included a bell "...whose sweet and solemn tones can be heard all over the town and for miles around."[108] The church's capacity was 800 worshippers.

The stained glass windows in St. Mary's bear the names of the founding families, like Sacca. "As a child, I thought you had to be an extremely good person to have a window. I never associated money or funding...and they are beautiful windows..."[109] Dona Ang Yates recalls.

Prior to 1921, when "...Mr. and Mrs. Frank Sacca were the

first family to...raise their family in the resort,"[110] few families made Ocean City their home year-round. Father Walter Knight, O.S.F.S., became pastor of both St. Francis DeSales in Salisbury and St. Mary Star of the Sea. "Other Catholic families were in Ocean City as merchants and spent many months at the resort each year."[111]

Dona Ang Yates, whose family moved to Worcester County from Pennsylvania, recalls that, in 1941:

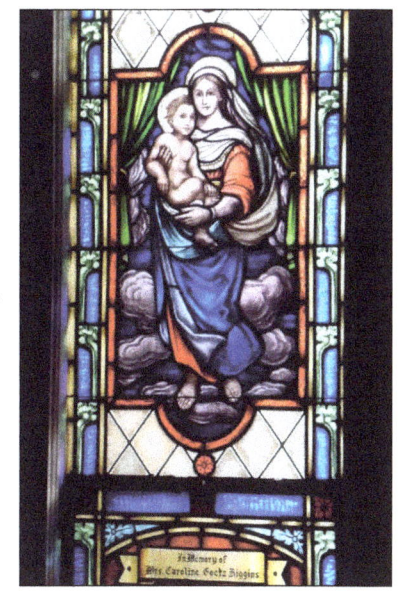

Stained glass window in St. Mary's
Photo by Ellen Marshall

> My mother, used to say that our family was one-third of the congregation when we first began attending St. Mary's...My father was not a Catholic, but he was very dedicated to making sure his children got to Mass...He was a travelling salesman... we had to get into Ocean City from Herring Creek along Golf Course Road...The teachers in the public school made fun of us being a Catholic 'Did you do your homework, or did you have to say the rosary'...they'd tease us.."[112]

By the 1950s, the Ocean City churches scheduled seven to nine Masses on Sunday. After the reforms of Vatican II, a 1962 - 1965 Council which made many reforms to the Church's approach to worship, a Mass was added on Saturday evening.

In 1967, the rapid growth of the resort necessitated that a mission church, Holy Savior, be erected at 16th Street and Philadelphia Avenue. During that time, St. Mary's was also expanded to seat 1300, and offered Masses at "7:00, 8:00, 9:00, 10:00, and 11:00 AM."[113] Father Stephen Connell, pastor, authorized adding colonnades on the front and sides of the Church. Holy Savior, which now shares the pastor with St. Mary's, was only open in the summer. "There was standing-room only...because it was at that time that 'condo row, as we call it' was growing in the late 60s and early 70s, people were standing 2 and 3 deep in the aisles, literally..."[114]

On her website, Dolores Monet recounts that:

> There used to be an elderly priest there, Monsignor Stout, while he said Mass, his Chesapeake Bay retrievers sat quietly in one of the isles near the front of the church."[115]

Other parishioners recount how sometimes those dogs, Pat and Mike, would interrupt one of Fr. Stout's sermons with their antics. One of them could be seen getting down on all fours and scrunching underneath the altar for a nap. Or they'd saunter up to Fr. Stout for a quick pet. During the summer, when Masses were full of beachgoers, even the visiting priests had to "adopt" the dogs. According to Dona Ang Yates:

> Fr. Stout would ask the visiting priests to take Pat and Mike for a walk. They didn't always like the chore. So, one of the younger priests discovered that one of the dogs was frightened by the sound of the popgun at the shooting gallery at Trimpers. So, he walked the dog up to the gallery and, I think

it was Mike, ran right back to the rectory. When the young priest arrived back, Fr. Stout asked the priest why Mike came back early. "Oh, Father, he missed you so much he ran straight back to see you."[116]

Another parishioner, Mary Lou Jones, recalls an encounter in the early 70s:

It was a Saturday and I was going to confession. It was kind of dark and I was kneeling there, at the back of church and I felt this presence, you know when you know someone's near you. And I turned and I was nose-to-nose with the dog...Scared me to death.[117]

Parishioners all remember Monsignor Stout with such affection. Mary Lou Jones, who was the director of religious education for the parish, sums it up:

Monsignor liked three things...he loved the Church and he loved God...he loved animals: he loved his dogs. He loved good food and he loved music. He was an accomplished pianist. 'He played at some of the weddings.' (Betsy Ludlam pipes in). One day I was in Salisbury...I went to the rectory. And I happened to look up ... the blinds were open – they had some kind of side room- and he was sitting there, playing...[118]

When I was young, our large Catholic family worshipped at St. Mary's on the Sunday[119] during our week of vacation. Many times, our family shared a pew with my aunts, uncles and cousins who were vacationing at the same time. As a young adult, we began going to Mass at Holy Savior because of a more convenient Mass time. Holy Savior is also the Church where my husband and I took our own children to worship, and many of those Sundays we went with brothers and sisters and their children. We used to joke that our home parish was transplanted 150 miles away!

Betsy Ludlam remembers that the Saturday midnight Mass became very popular with residents and those on vacation. "We could go out and then stop off at Holy Savior Church to attend Mass. We had competition from the clubs across Coastal Highway ... it was just jam-packed."[120]

As vacationers started to invest in condominiums far from 17th Street, Ocean City's church-going population migrated also. There are now five Catholic Churches between St. Mary's and St. Andrew's on 144th Street. Mary Lou Jones recalls that "...from the day St. Luke's opened (at 100th Street), it has been full..."[121]

Betsy Ludlam, who at the time served on the Parish Council, recounts a period when "The Bishop...wanted to tear St. Mary's down. Parking was an issue, structural problems with an older building, etc. Fr. Connell was very upset – that was in the late '70s...when they restored the Church...."[122] instead of demolishing all of that history or moving St. Mary's to another location. Today St. Mary's Star of the Sea is open, operates year-round and "the people who worship at St. Mary's... it's kind of become its own group ...it's this feeling of family," Mary Lou Jones observes.[123] When one looks at the beautiful stained glass windows, or the brass candlesticks, one can soak in the history and the sacrifices of the early Ocean City residents who built the Church.

The Church also continues to be the focus of family celebrations. Mary Lou Jones was happy that her twin girls, who were baptized at St. Mary's, wanted to be married there. It turned out that both ceremonies took place at St. Mary's, two weeks apart. "They were both gorgeous weddings,"[124] Mary Lou continued.

Betsy Ludlam observed that:

> My wedding took place at St. Mary's...Many parishioners, who were brought up in St. Mary's want to be married there...It is so quaint ...Two of my four daughters were married at St. Mary's...My parents were buried from St. Mary's...there's a lot of history and memories there."[125]

Every Thanksgiving, St. Mary's sponsors an ecumenical service for residents of all faiths.

*Betsey Ludlam and Mary Lou Jones at interview.
Photo by Ellen Marshall*

Crisis of conscience averted. There was no longer an excuse to skip Mass while vacationing. Starting with the late 19th century, St. Mary Star of the Sea would be joined by other Christian churches like St. Paul's.

St. Paul's By-The-Sea Episcopal Church

The Catholic Church's religious kissing cousin, the Episcopal Church,[126] also began its building campaign in the late 19th century. Stephen Taber and his wife, wealthy Long Island businesspeople who owned thousands of acres on Sinepuxent Bay, donated the site. Bishop Henry C. Lay of the Protestant Episcopal Diocese of Easton began construction of a church in the spring of 1881. That land, combined with a donated parcel from Colonel William B.R. Selby, was the site of St. Paul's. This new Episcopal chapel was planned to front the west side of Baltimore Avenue between South 1st and South 2nd Streets, directly behind Congress Hall.[127]

In *A Century of Celebration: St. Paul's By The Sea Episcopal Church Ocean City, Maryland* the author captures the place of St. Paul's in the early history of the resort.

> As the population increased on the Eastern Shore, new towns and areas of population began to emerge. Interest heightened on the development of a barrier island resort, later known as Ocean City, located seven miles east of Berlin, including Colonel Lemuel Showell, who already had a small cottage of the island... The history of St. Paul's by-the-Sea Episcopal Church closely parallels the development of Ocean City itself. Many of the founding families of Ocean City are also the founding families of our church.[128]

Until construction was completed, congregants held services at the Atlantic Hotel and Congress Hall. In fact, the first record of Episcopal religious services in Ocean City was August 12, 1877, when Bishop Lay "preached twice to large and delighted Audiences in the parlor of the Atlantic Hotel."[129]

That church building gave only short service because church leaders wanted it to be relocated in the newly thriving north area: some called it "up the beach." Mr. and Mrs. John Waggaman of Washington, D.C. gave Rev. J. Gibson Gantt two parcels of land on the northeast corner of Baltimore Avenue and North 3rd Street. Ms. Bradford explains:

> It was considered instrumental to the success of the church to secure land...as the trek through the sand to the small chapel across from the Congress Hotel (the present site of Adolfo's Restaurant) was undesirable to those 'dressed for church.' The original church building and lot sale went into the construction kitty for the newer St. Paul's.[130]

Many of the founders of the expansion of Ocean City served on the subscription committee. Mrs. John Showell, owner of the Ocean Swell cottages, was one.

Fr. John R. Royner, rector of St. Paul's, Worcester Parish, Berlin, conducted the first services in the new building. The founding families of St. Paul were considered "transient," the church sat 300 persons, and was valued at $2,000.[131] In 1894, Rev. David Howard, rector of St. Paul's, Berlin, was the first recorded Minister-in-Charge. However, like St. Mary's Catholic Church, St. Paul's was an adjunct to an existing Church in the diocese, and the two shared one pastor. At that point in Ocean City's history, there were few permanent residents; certainly not enough to warrant a full-time clerical presence.

That status changed in 1920. St. Paul's by-the-Sea became an independent parish of the Diocese of Easton.

The original structure was likely damaged or destroyed[132] by the Storm of 1933, the same storm that created the inlet. Before its destruction, that building was used for commercial storage.[133]

Wednesday, November 21, 1962, was an ominous day for the downtown area, where many structures were built of clapboard. A fire broke out at the Plimhimmon Hotel. The then-mayor, Hugh Cropper, was quoted as saying:

> I wouldn't have given five cents for the rest of the property in the next couple of blocks. I thought that a good deal of this town would go up in flames.[134]

The strategy adopted by the firefighters battling the blaze was to intentionally set fire to nearby buildings, including St. Paul's. The "congregation scrambled to remove valuable artifacts from the Church...The firemen eventually gained the upper hand and St. Paul's was spared..."[135]

The congregation at St. Paul's shares an interesting connection to the Catholic Church. Bishop Alfred Curtis, who succeeded Bishop Becker of the Wilmington Diocese, was a convert from the Episcopal Church.[136] He grew up in Dorchester County, also on the Eastern Shore of Maryland, and later donated money to the Church for its construction.

St. Paul's by-the-Sea held various fundraisers to support its programs. One of those ventures started in 1941 later grew into "Antiques-By-The-Sea." This annual event, held at the Roland E. Powell Convention Center, is "one of the longest-running annual shows of its kind in the country."[137]

For a time during the 1960s, St. Paul's also sponsored a theater company, Lighthouse Players. *The Solid Gold Cadillac*, its premiere production, had been on Broadway. The Players presented the show on March 2 and 3, 1961, in the auditorium of the Elementary School.[138]

The Church of the Holy Spirit Episcopal

The town of Ocean City expanded its borders from 41st Street to the Delaware State line in 1965. The Reverend William L. Dewees, rector of St. Paul's, located a lot on Coastal Highway and 100th Street as a possible site for another church. James Caine, a local developer, donated the land for a new Episcopal church.

Until construction was complete, worshipers met at a temporary chapel on 72nd Street. They used the altar and cross from the original church and an organ donated by St. Paul's organist, Jack Caldwell.

Reverend Dewees presided at the first service at Holy Spirit on June 23, 1968.[139] By 1985, Holy Spirit began offering year-round services. It evolved into a self-sustaining parish of the Easton Episcopal Diocese in 1991.

Ministries of St. Paul's By-The-Sea

The Women's Guild was the driving force behind the fundraising events for St. Paul's. Mrs. Marian Cropper, who came to Ocean City and St. Paul's in 1946, was first a member of the Junior Guild, St. Claire's. Mrs. Cropper recalls:

> The Guild became very active during Fr. DeWees's pastorship. He was Ocean City's favorite minister,

not just to St. Paul's members, but to everyone. One of the Guild's prominent members, Mrs. Sally Purnell, who owned the Atlantic Hotel, hosted "Antiques-by-the-Sea," a very large and popular event, first at the hotel. Mrs. Purnell and Daisy Townsend were early co-chairs of the event.[140]

Mrs. Elizabeth Showell Strohecker, known as "Mama," was the inspiration behind the Antique Show "which from its inception in the early 40s has been one of the main sources of 'outside income.'"[141] Mrs. Strohecker was also the first woman to be elected to the Vestry of the Church. Among other craft items and gift items, the women of the Guild sold crewel pillows, table linens, and aprons, both at the antiques show and the pre-Christmas Bazaar. Mrs. Cropper recalls that people came from all over to that bazaar each year.

Reverend David Dingwall, St. Paul's pastor starting in 2005, was proud of his community's long history of service. He explained that the DeWees Community Center, attached to the Church and facing 3rd Street, is the site of various classes and activities open to the community. "…As Ocean City grew, the need for assistance, especially during the summer months, was apparent…many young priests… would spend a month in Ocean City…assisting with services."[142] The church named the programs Red Door, because of the recognizable entrance to the Center, which everyone identified as the gateway to the Church's ministries.

While tending to his church's mission, Father Dingwall noted the strong smell of smoke. The entire rectory structure became quickly engulfed in flames. Father remembered that his laptop, containing much of St. Paul's records was upstairs.

He went in to retrieve it and it was there that he succumbed to the fire.

Atlantic United Methodist

The original Methodist church is located at 4th Street and Baltimore and was founded in 1915. As recalled in a 2005 church publication:

> At a meeting held April 25, 1915 a resolution was passed requesting the Wilmington Conference to establish a Methodist Church in Ocean City and to send a pastor to serve. The Conference responded by appointing Charles W. Spry as Pastor. He received $650 as salary the first year. The name selected for our church was First Methodist Episcopal Church of Ocean City. When the name changed to Atlantic Methodist is not known but it may have not been until 1940 after unification of the three branches of Methodism.[143]

I mentioned in an earlier chapter that the full-time residents are hard-working. They also have historically been dedicated to their churches. As evidenced from their beautiful houses of worship, parishioners see religion as a central force in their lives. All three of the larger historic churches – Catholic, Episcopal and Methodist – have

The original church was built across the street from its present location on Baltimore Avenue and 3rd Street. Like St. Mary's and St. Paul's by-the-Sea, Atlantic United Methodist's founders were many of the early Ocean City pioneers and businesspersons. Founding family names include the following: Thomas Coffin and Clinton T. Coffin, relatives of

Isaac Coffin, the first rooming house owner; John J. Gibbs, Jr, James Gibbs and William Gibbs, owner of the Breakers Hotel and Dough Rollers, Inc.; John C. Cropper, W.A. Cropper, C.P. Cropper , and Hugh Cropper, family of early rooming house owners; I.S. Mumford, and James H. Mumford, early fishing camp and related industries: Sam L. Quillen, Jr, William J. Quillen, Ezra Bunting, fishing boats, who helped to build a robust fishing and rental fishing boat industry which still operates ; Mr. and Mrs. Hastings, Josephine Hastings, Kendall Hastings, Florence Hastings, and George Edwin Hastings, of the S.M. Hastings family who bought original shares of the Atlantic Hotel Company and later built the Shoreham Hotel; George H. Powell and Della K. Powell who bought the historic Atlantic Hotel from Dr. Townsend ; G.B. Dennis, family of Ella Dennis who bought one of the original lots of the Atlantic Hotel Company and operated the Dennis Hotel, one of the early lodgings; and George Massey, descendent of Samuel Massey and Josephine Hastings, who with Isaac Coffin operated small hotels in a growing Ocean City hospitality industry.

As the congregation grew, it became necessary to plan for a new church. That structure was dedicated in 1963. We read in the 90th anniversary publication:

> A. A. Hensel Fink was awarded the contract for the architecture and George B. Cropper, Inc. was awarded the contract to build the church. Groundbreaking services were held March 4, 1962 and services for the laying of the cornerstone were held August 26, 1962.[144]

Another important date in the Church's history was the dedication of a new Schantz Pipe organ on April 14, 1991. At-

Atlantic Methodist Episcopal Church circa 1950
Courtesy of Church archives

lantic Methodist's ministries include a thrift shop, a Haiti Mission team, Helping Hands, and Hands Up, offering help to the homeless.

Atlantic Methodist currently has an active membership of about 750 which, of course, grows appreciably during the summer vacation months. During that time of year, the pastors conduct service on the beach in front of Shenanigan's restaurant each Sunday. Because Shenanigans is owned by a member family, they are willing to turn the space in front of their Irish pub into a hallowed space to draw in the shorts crowd. This worship service is in keeping with their evangelization goals to reach out to youth at the resort. Like any other kids away from home, they also enjoy the comfort of worship that they choose for themselves.

Longtime member June Todd recalls what makes her church unique:

Inside Atlantic Methodist
Photo by Ellen Marshall

> Well, when the Church started it had many of the founding families of Ocean City as members... it's the people who make us unique. ...Our current focus is on joining with the other Churches to help out residents who run out of food money. For example, United Methodist members hand out bags of food twice a week... and offer clothing through its thrift shop, which is open every day except Sunday.[145]

Parishioners Jack Moore and June Todd talk about the ecumenical cooperation among the Ocean City churches:

> There are ecumenical services during the year. A Good Friday Sunrise Service on the boardwalk led by the pastors each year...Thanksgiving Dinner is attended by members of all the Churches... At the death of Father David Dingwall, they had a combined choir at the memorial service...[146]

United Methodist welcomed its first female pastor, Patty Frick, on July 1, 2014. Pastor Frick follows a distinguished group of 30 former pastors who have served the Church over its 99-year history.

St. Martin's

Although St. Mary's was the first church in Ocean City, its origin dates almost 100 years behind another Christian church, St. Martin's of Showell, 13 miles NW of the resort. St. Martin's was constructed in durable brick in northern Worcester County and has outlasted many newer churches.

Michael Morgan tells us that "By the middle of the eighteenth century, northern Worcester County was finally attracting enough colonists to warrant the building of a permanent church."[147] In 1765, St. Martin's was the first church built in northern Worcester County. Existing churches like the Episcopal Cathedral in Easton and St. Francis de Sales in Salisbury helped to support the new Christian denominations on the lower shore at their beginnings.

The First Presbyterian Church in Ocean City

In 1892, the First Presbyterian Church opened its doors as a Union Sunday School. When it opened the church on North Division Street, it cost $1,000 to build. Like other Christian denominations in Ocean City who were founded before the resort population settled year-round, First Presbyterian was opened under the auspices of another church, the Buckingham Presbyterian Church of Berlin.

Representatives of the Presbytery met on April 4, 1909, with 34 charter members to form the existing church. Prior to this meeting, worship places were "...a series of buildings, including a saloon..."[148] Eventually a manse was added to house the pastor. First Presbyterian's original church was purchased and converted for use as a Baptist church.

When the Presbytery bought four lots at 13th Street and Philadelphia in 1955, the present church was erected at a cost of $225,000. Its first worship service was held on June 16, 1963, and the congregation built a new manse in February 1966.

The architect, following the recommendations of the congregation, designed the interior of the new church in the shape of an inverted boat. Were they signaling that the church is a vehicle on the sea of life? Another tongue-in-cheek reference to the Bible in First Presbyterian is the design of the roof, shaped as if it were an inverted Noah's Ark.

Son Spot

An informal beach resort also deserves an informal ministry. One such worship space is Son Spot at 12 Worcester Street, just off the boardwalk. It is operated by members of the Spirit Life Full Gospel Church. No permanent pastor has ever served this congregation. Members volunteer to preside at services in which they share faith experiences.

One of Son Spot's most visible ministry is a food outreach to the thousands of international students who work at the beach during the summer. Like all churches in Ocean City, off-season attendance varies. During the summer months, Son Spot can grow to 1,000 worshippers.[149]

Temple Bat Yam

Ocean City and its environs are home to an increasing

Jewish population. The website "At the Beach" lists three synagogues on the Delmarva Peninsula: Beth Israel Conservative Synagogue in Salisbury, Temple Bat Yam in Berlin, and Ahavat Shalom in Ocean City.

Temple Bat Yam describes itself as "...a Reform Jewish congregation committed to the ideals and truths of Judaism and to maintaining the traditions and lessons of our rich heritage while respecting the realities and integrity of interfaith marriages and interfaith families..."[150]

Rabbi Susan Warsaw leads the TBY community. They offer Shabbat services every Friday at 8:00 PM and Saturdays at 9:30 AM. After Saturday worship, they engage in Torah study and discussion. The Temple practices Tzedakah, a practice of allocating a portion of earnings to the Temple. They support a hospice, collect paperbacks for the military, and supply food for the Shepherd's Crook at St. Paul-by-the-Sea. Temple Bat Yam also schedules many events during the year for the benefit of their membership and the greater Delmarva Peninsula.

St. Peter's Lutheran

In 1980 this church was established by pastor Rudolph Barr on Coastal Highway. Like other denominations, this faith community met at the Ocean City Convention Center while they raised money and prepared for construction.

Other Worship Spaces

Having the support of a religious family has been an important cultural value through the millennia. The form of that worship evolved with social and spiritual change. Ocean

City moved along with those trends by expanding beyond the traditional faith groups.

A prime example is the meditation moment created by those stopping at the sand sculptures created by Randy Hoffman since 1981. The themes of the sculptures carved in the sand at the boardwalk between 1st and 2nd Streets are based on Holy Scripture passages. Hoffman calls it his sand ministry, supported by donations dropped into his "collection basket." There is no sermon unless one stops to discuss the verse with him or other passers-by.

Several non-denominational churches have sprung up in the resort community. Christian Outreach at 60th Street; Trinity Church, a Charismatic Episcopal congregation which meets at Showell Elementary School, as does Fellowship Alliance; Assembly of God, west of Ocean City. These demonstrate the variety of faith groups in existence today. A Mennonite community, CrossWay Church, holds meetings on

Face of Compassion by Randy Hoffman
Photo courtesy of David Sites

Ocean Gateway in Ocean City. Other congregations have likewise grown up along the other nearby Delmarva beaches.

Whether one worships in a building with a community or looks inward for communicating with a Higher Being, the beach at Ocean City seems to awaken connections. One of the shared connections of this beach town is enjoying some memorable characters.

Footprints in the sand
Photo by unsplash.com user Abdolazim Mollaie

Iconic Characters

*"Twenty years from now you will be more disappointed by the things that you didn't do than by the ones you did do. So throw away the bowlines. Sail away from the safe harbor. Catch the trade winds in your sails.
Explore. Dream. Discover..."*

Mark Twain

Boardwalk entertainment in Ocean City comes in all shapes and sizes. You can be entranced by people watching from a porch-front rocking chair. Also the numerous wannabe famous musicians and entertainers on the boardwalk make Ocean City supremely engaging. The salt air and slow-motion state of mind at a beach community seem to grow their share of iconic characters.

Boardwalk Elvis strummed and gyrated every night at different places. During the 70s Roy Beckett played a kazoo while standing on his head. Then there was Tex in his ten-gallon hat, and the team of banjo-playing Shorty and his dog, Mandy. Teens and young adults working at the resort for the summer play guitars, flutes, slide trombones, and keyboards, hoping to make a few dollars to supplement their minimum-wage day jobs.

Talk to anyone who knows Ocean City and they will tell you the town's character has been shaped by its memorable residents. George Hurley, a life-long resident and historian, describes how the Eastern Shore mentality likely came about: "the slow pace and ease of living created a personality most regard as very sociable, but plainspoken, with a touch of salt."[151]

When I sit on a boardwalk bench or lean out of my hotel window, I can hear that directness in the conversations among locals:

> First voice: Humph, too many changes since last year. What happened to the Lambros's place?
>
> Second voice: Bit the dust just like all the other old hotels we grew up with. What are they trying to do? Create another Atlantic City? Just ain't like it used to be.

First voice: City folk think we need to move with the times. Weren't nothing wrong with this town until, who was that again, Bobby Baker? Too many trying to make a buck off of what our granddaddies started.

Second voice: Yep. We learned early – just takes good old-fashioned work and a bit of luck. Now, take that crazy guy with the signs all around his place....

My interviews with Ocean City residents and businesspersons confirm that it took a lot of chutzpah to first recognize that this laid-back beach community could become a destination. And anyone in the travel industry will tell you that several well-remembered characters help to bring many of us back, year after year.

Joe Kro-Art

If you have been going to OC since the 1970s, you will remember the Ocean Gallery commercials. In one of them, Joe puts a dummy on a motorcycle on the gallery roof, uses a pulley system to "drive" the bike onto the beach, and then, in the final shot, lies on his back with his arms and legs up, dressed in his tuxedo. Upon recounting that shoot story, Joe explains that he did not apply for a permit to shoot on the boardwalk. But, when airing the commercial brought some notice to the beach town, all was good with the city fathers.

That's Joe Kro-Art (hyphenated name, his idea, not his parents) in a nutshell.

John Lewis fills us in on the humble beginnings of Joe Kro-Art in Ocean City:

While still at Towson (State University), he went to Ocean City during the summer of 1963 with a car full of his paintings (landscapes, still lifes, abstracts) and a notion of selling them to tourists. He found a sympathetic landlord who rented him a space, a former chicken carryout, at Baltimore and Caroline streets, for 20 percent of whatever he sold.

"All I had to do was sell something, and I'd be ahead," says Kro-Art, grinning at the memory. "I didn't sell much, but I survived. And I established the first Ocean Gallery.[152]

Ocean Gallery is just that – a gallery, a viewing place, inside and out. You can find anything from fine and original art to a Marx Brothers movie poster in Joe's place. An Aubrey Bodine classic photo print or a Paul DeRemegis pastel of a local iconic landmark, like Memorial Stadium, is just as comfortable alongside Mick Jagger's open mouth with its protruding tongue. The slapdash way old building materials are affixed to the building's exterior makes millions of people grin, stop, look and enter. And that is just the effect Joe set out to create. "Art should be fun," Kro-Art tells me.

Lewis sums up his impressions of Ocean Gallery's genius:

But in all the chaos, two things tend to go unnoticed about Kro-Art: He is a shrewd businessman and a serious artist himself. But you'd need to visit him at home in Monkton to get a sense of that.[153]

Joe spends part of his summer weeks at the Ocean away from his Monkton farm, away from his own opportunities to ply his craft. Those visitors from across the world or down

Ocean Gallery in all its glory
Photo by Eugene Marshall

the boardwalk visitors to Ocean Gallery will usually find Joe at the front of the store, watching the smiles. He revels in people's reactions to his unusual take on the art world. When asked, Joe interprets those reactions as an art form in itself and places mirrors around the entrance and cash register to record the glee, if even for a moment.

Ocean Gallery has been the inspiration for numerous blog posts, films and articles. A March 2013 article in *View*, the German equivalent of *People Magazine*, details compliments of the unusual gallery. Ocean Gallery enjoys much ink in *The Sun* and former *City Paper*, both Baltimore dailies, as well as tourist sites. A scene from *Ping-Pong Summer*, an indie film starring Susan Sarandon, helped to bring international attention to this quirky art venue. Joe Kro-Art, a master marketer, is largely responsible for the gallery's widespread notoriety.

"Live out of your imagination, not your history," Steven Covey advises successful people. Joe Kro-Art seems to have discovered that wisdom.

Zippy Lewis

Ocean City is one of those places that seems to spawn outrageous characters. What is not known about them is invented, or at least hyperbolized. Perhaps it's the water. Zipporah Lewis, a 19th century widow whose picture hangs on the lobby walls of the Dunes Manor Hotel, is a character well-known to locals.

Legends about Mrs. Zipporah Lewis seem to have followed her during life and continue after her death. From a simple existence that began in Delaware you see what life must have been before Ocean City became a destination. What we do know about her is that she was married to a sailor; together, they had five children and she eventually moved onto land near the Delaware border. Like many persons who seemed to live very ordinary lives, Zippy's persona was made memorable by Ocean City residents' stories.

The Zippy Lewis house was located bayside of what is known as Devil's Island between 117th and 118th Streets. When earlier investors thought that they could not make a successful use of their land, some of these tracts reverted back to Wicomico County for unpaid taxes. Zipporah Lewis, from 1856 to 1858, owned three of those tracts of land.

When Zippy's husband did not return from a sea voyage, locals saw her searching the horizon for sight of his ship every day. Mr. Lewis's ship disappeared sometime between

1846 and the 1850 census record, where Mrs. Lewis is identified as head of household. A creative person, Zippy used the lumber and driftwood that washed up with the tide to build her house on the beach.

Mrs. Lewis's family income seems to have been earned through sales of what she scavenged from shipwreck "treasures" that washed up on the beach. Her portrait is haunting, a windswept attractive young woman intently watching what we can surmise is the high seas.

Portrait of Zipporah Lewis which hangs in the lobby of the Dunes Manor Hotel

The Trimpers

Daniel and Margaret Trimper are a German couple who immigrated to Ocean City in 1890. They headed an enterprising boardwalk family with seven surviving children, eight grandchildren, and numerous great-grandchildren. Three Trimpers went on to serve as city councilmen and mayors. They were typical of the early Ocean City families, who built the resort with hard work and a clear vision.

Daniel Trimper began his family's 120-year boardwalk presence with a small carousel outside of an establishment he ran on the boardwalk. His greatest purchase, the one that continues to delight children of all ages today, is that Herschell-Spillman carousel decorated in the trompe l'oeil style.

In an article on the 100th anniversary of the park, we read:

A view of the Herschell--Spillman 1912 carousel at Trimper's Rides on the OC Boardwalk. Photograph by Ellen Marshall

Rebuilding the Sea Bright in 1900 following a severe storm, the Trimpers modeled the new structure on Great Britain's Windsor Castle. The two hotels together with a theater and an amusement park thus became known as Windsor Resort.[154]

A 1912 purchase[155] also adds to the historic significance of Trimper's Rides. It was that year that Daniel Trimper purchased a massive carousel from the Herschell-Spillman Company in North Tonawanda, NY. The carousel was 50 feet in diameter and was unique because it was only one of two made by the firm. The other was in Coney Island, New York and that one was later destroyed by fire.

The merry-go-round's forty-five animals, three chariots, and one rocking chair were driven by a steam engine; rides originally cost just a nickel. One hundred years later, the ride now electrified costs you six points. Another option is to buy the discounted package of forty points for thirty dollars. Classified as one of the oldest still-operating carousels in the nation, generations of families come every year to ride their favorite animals. Smaller children tend to prefer the horses, but many choose their own steed from among a menagerie of cat, dog, frog, rooster, deer, goat, lion, tiger, ostrich, pig, or dragon.

Over the years the Trimpers added numerous rides; several of these rides also offer historic significance, such as a smaller carousel and a kiddie Ferris wheel which date to the 1920s. All the rides are kept in excellent working condition. If it were not for the gilt ornateness and beautiful hand-carved craftsmanship, you would find it difficult to believe that parents and grandparents once rode the same rides. Today those same families are now bringing their offspring to do the same.

The Trimpers keep the carousel well maintained. Every off-season Antoinette Bruno meticulously examines each carousel figure, restores any damaged parts, and repaints. Bruno, the daughter of Daniel Trimper II, was the president of Windsor Resort Corporation until March 2020.

The Trimpers boast a long history of public service. Daniel Trimper's son, Daniel, Jr., took over the Windsor Resort Corporation after his father's death. He was also elected mayor of Ocean City for four terms. A great-grandson, Daniel IV, served on City Council and eventually became Council President. Grandson Granville D. Trimper served on the City Council for 18 years, many of those as Council President; he also served as Mayor. Granville also served on the Worcester

County Commissioners as President for 4 years. He became the corporation's manager in 1980. Shantytown Village was developed by Daniel Trimper IV. The Ocean City Dispatch tells readers that it "was designed to resemble a New England fishing village and was modeled on photos taken by Trimper during a visit to Nantucket Island."[156]

The Bunting and Powell Families

Ocean City's full story cannot be told without talking about its fishermen. From the time visitors entering OC from the Route 50 bridge get their first glimpse of the Bay and Ocean, they see anglers casting their lines into the Bay. Restaurants, like the Angler and Harrison's Harbor Watch, feature local seafood. Fishing piers line the Sinepuxent Bay. Three families, the Buntings, the Powells and the Purnells, continue to play a major role in the development of this coastal paradise.

Michael Morgan talks about the end of the 19th century when fishing became king:

> When Christopher Ludlam came to town, however, he was more interested in establishing pathways for fish than the roadways that humans took...In the 1880s ...He knew that large schools of fish migrated along the beach within several hundred yards of the breakers... Ludlam had a series of pilings driven into the ocean floor a short distance from the beach. He used these posts to string a system of nets that funneled the fish into a large holding area...pound fishermen used sturdy boats that would return to shore heavily laden with today's catch."[157]

The Bunting family, which owns the Angler Restaurant and its fishing and boating business, first came to Ocean City at the turn of the 20th century. Charles R. Bunting, Sr, was an early fishing pioneer. Charles bought the Angler. His son, Talbot, operated a fishing business off the Talbot Street pier.

Dale Timmons recounts that:

> The creation of the inlet was a natural disaster that allowed Ocean City to become a fishing destination and it spurred a whole new industry in the form of offshore and nearshore charter fishing... The fish that propelled Ocean City into international recognition is the white marlin and the resort became known as "The White Marlin Capital of the World."[158]

Bunting Fishing Classic
www.angleroc.com

Captain Levin Bunting operated a business chartering small boats to vacationers in the early 20th century. The boats were docked near the present site of the Ocean City Life-Saving Station Museum off Sinepuxent Bay. He also owned the Princeton, a 45-foot vessel which could carry upwards of two dozen passengers. Today's descendants of Charles, Talbot, and Levin run a restaurant at the heart of downtown, offer a boat tour, and operate docks.

"Fish" Powell

During his tenure as Ocean City's Mayor, everyone knew Roland Powell from his walks down the boardwalk or appearances on local TV. The man born in Ocean City started off as a lifeguard, then a city councilman, real estate entrepreneur, firefighter, and eventually Mr. Mayor. Throughout his life, Powell was a promoter *par excellence* of the city he loved. Former Ocean City Emergency Management Director Clay Stamp recalled growing up in the fire company with Powell as its leader:

> It was from a young man's eyes as a 14-year-old fire cadet that I first laid eyes on Fire Chief Fish Powell," he said. "Salty, squared away, with a cigar in the corner of his mouth and donning a brilliant white fire chief's helmet, barking out short, concise orders to many who followed them to bring an emergency situation under control. Later, as a volunteer firefighter and an Ocean City paramedic, emergency manager and eventually as director of emergency services, I learned how to become a leader from lessons learned from great men who

served in the Ocean City Volunteer Fire Company and largely from Fish Powell.[159]

It was Fish Powell who was able to marshal all the necessary resources after a major hurricane to set the stage for Ocean City's transition to a year-round resort. Once again, Mother Nature remade the landscape – beach and boardwalk. With investments, Powell was able to plan a protective dune system, erect a sea wall along the boardwalk, and plan for beach replenishment every four years. Besides funding, it took multiple layers of cooperation and inspiring other government officials to get it done.

Bill Purnell

I found Mr. Purnell at his early-morning haunt, Layton's. After I started going to the Ocean to conduct interviews and ate breakfast at the iconic restaurant, I noticed a group of men sitting at tables pushed together in a long row. One day I asked my waitress, "Who are these guys?"

Her response was, "They are here every day and include some of our famous locals." That trip I had planned to try to track down Bill Purnell, owner of the famed Atlantic Hotel.

"Is one of them Mr. Purnell, Bill Purnell?" I inquired.

"Yes, he is that gentleman," she pointed him out.

So I walked over to the remaining group of guys and asked Mr. Purnell if he would be willing to give me 20 minutes to a half-hour for an interview for this book. Mr. Purnell graciously agreed and came over to my table. I soon discovered that Bill Purnell loved to talk about his Ocean City. Wow, I love this town!

Much of the substance of our chat is included in the hotel

chapter. Mr. Purnell was engaging, funny and told one story after another. He explained that his pride in what he and his family had accomplished is mixed with concerns about losing the essence of the resort, the family-friendly ambience.

What struck me about the man is that he exemplified what George Hurley had told me about the people of Ocean City: very sociable, but plainspoken, with a touch of salt. Some of Bill's descriptions were, shall I say, unprintable.

Bobby Baker

Ocean City development really took off when investors saw the potential of building properties further up Coastal Highway. An iconic actor in this move was Robert Gene Baker, known as Bobby.

Yohoho and a Bottle of Rum
Photo by Eugene Marshall

The hurricane of 1962 opened up many opportunities for expansion. For example, water and power made it possible to continue development. George Hurley witnessed the influence of the Bay Bridge's opening in 1952 and the opportunity to get federal disaster money to lay pipes and power lines. Many construction jobs and related industries provided employment for residents. The influx of federal funding, Hurley states, was partially due to Bobby Baker's Washington connections.

Mr. Baker became part of the group that built the Carousel Oceanfront Hotel & Condos in 1962. According to a local article at the time of Baker's death:

> The former top staffer for Senate Democratic majority and fixer for Lyndon Johnson built it (The Carousel) with partners in the barren sands north of 118th Street. He opened it in 1962 and did it on loans (51 between 1959 and 1963) piled on top of loans while making less than $20,000 a year in the Senate.[160]

In an interview with *The Washington Post* Bobby Baker, then a legislative aide to Lyndon Johnson, explained his success:

> As they (members of Congress) took advantage of privileged information to get on the ground floor of attractive investments, so did I. As they used their powerful positions to gain loans or credit otherwise might not have been granted, so did I.[161]

But Mr. Baker's boasting eventually resulted in a fall from grace. He spent 15 months in prison in 1971 after a conviction of tax evasion, bribery and fraud.[162]

Boardwalk Elvis

Those of us who spend time in Ocean City loved to see some of the must-see sights on the boardwalk. One of our favorite memories was watching the performance of Boardwalk Elvis, aka Norman Webb of Showell.

Reportedly, Mr. Webb drove his bike from Showell, a 13 mile trip to OC to do what he loved – perform. Karra Hallisseau tells us:

> It was always a special moment when you saw "Elvis" walking down the boardwalk. He'd be wearing either his black, white or red jumpsuit, carrying his boombox on his shoulder, and playing the kazoo along with the Elvis music coming out of the speakers.[163]

A *Baltimore Sun* article chronicles Boardwalk Elvis's performance style:

> He walks the boards on weekends...making his way up and down the boards with his boombox, singing along with an Elvis tape... dressed like Elvis in his Vegas days...and has been doing this as long as anyone remembers.[164]

"The city should subsidize him, " says Mr. Tim Gilbert in the article. " He's just always been a part of the landscape, like the beach, the sand. He's always been there."

Elvis lives in so many impersonators, but we lost Mr. Webb in 2020.

Roy Becket

"Vanishing Ocean City," a column in the *Maryland Coast Dispatch*, wrote:

One of the most popular characters in the 1970s was Roy Beckett whose claim to fame was playing a kazoo while standing on his head. Roy lived with his sister in Snow Hill and would catch a daily ride to Ocean City where in addition to performing his act on the Boardwalk he worked for Hall's Restaurant.

Roy Beckett has not been seen for many years, but his legend lives on as part of "Vanishing Ocean City." It is a certainty that other unique and interesting characters will always be around to entertain future Boardwalk visitors.[165]

Randy Hoffman
Photo courtesy of David Sites

Everyone smiles at the beach.
Photo by Ellen Marshall

Afterthoughts

Henrietta and her chicks survived the great storm which changed this Atlantic paradise forever. Her offspring pepper their Ocean City today, providing great action photos for us as they go after a meal. Seagulls and humans agree that there is nothing like time spent downee oshun, hon.[166]

My happy place, Ocean City, Maryland, is shared by millions of others. What it means to me – family, traditions, relaxation, togetherness, creativity – also reflects the experience of others. The interviews woven into this book, the website, and social media reflections of so many and the other Ocean City books published verify that this Atlantic paradise is a jewel to be discovered and cherished.

My richest memories of doing research for this book are the interviews. Every Ocean City resident shared generously how important it was to them to invest their time, money and talent into this resort. Those investments paid off for some monetarily, but for many others simply knowing Ocean City would thrive is their reward.

I recall vividly the enthusiasm of George Hurley as he spoke about his Ocean City life. George's devotion to its history and culture and his rich observations of the people were contagious. Although George is no longer physically with us, his writings will keep Ocean City's past vibrant.

As long as the grit and determination of the hotel owners and other businesspersons remains strong, this Atlantic paradise will delight future generations of beach lovers. The historic family-owned hotels and restaurants in the downtown district will be replaced eventually. But the imprint they will leave is indelible.

Even while developers might erect more modern hotels and eateries along the Ocean and Bay, much of what created this Atlantic paradise remains true. It is as if the blood and sweat of the earliest entrepreneurs will forever flavor the culture of this unique place away.

Background Information

"Truth crushed to earth shall rise."
William Cullen Bryant

The Magic of the Surf
Photo by Eugene Marshall

Acknowledgements

It was important to me to use the voices of others who share my love for Ocean City. Thanks to the following Ocean City residents and visitors who generously gave so much of their time, knowledge, insights, and experiences during interviews:

George Hurley – Mr. Hurley was one of my first interviewees and he shared valuable information and insights into the resort's history. He was a city council member, county council commissioner, teacher, business owner, and historian. George and his wife Suzanne founded the Ocean City Life-Saving Station Museum. George died on August 9, 2015. Sue left us the following year.

Sandy Hurley – Sandy is the former curator of the Ocean City Life-Saving Station Museum. Sandy set up the interview meeting with her father-in-law. She also pointed out the highlights of the Museum's collections, in person and virtually.

Father David Dingwell – Father David, the former pastor of St. Paul's by-the-Sea Episcopal Church, was so generous with his time when I interviewed him a few months before the fire in which he lost his life. Father David had copied relevant portions of his church's archives for me. The archives were stored on that same laptop that he went back into the rectory to retrieve when he succumbed to smoke.

Father Stanislao Esposito – Father Stanislao, former pastor of St. Mary's Star of the Sea and Holy Savior opened his Church's archives to me. The documents included rich history of the beginnings of the Catholic Church in Ocean City.

Joe Kro-Art – Joe, owner of the Ocean World Gallery on the Boardwalk is an artist and master promoter of art for art's sake. Joe exudes enthusiasm for all forms of artistic expression.

Bill Purnell – Bill comes from a long line of owners of the Atlantic Hotel, the first hotel in Ocean City. His rich story telling of the town's highlights from the 1930s forward gave me insight into the OC culture.

Bill Gibbs – Bill, who with his wife owns the Dough Roller Restaurants and the Breakers Hotel, shared great memories of growing up in Ocean City and the storm of 1962. Bill died on October 2, 2021.

Anna Bushnell Dolle – Anna is the co-owner (with her brother) of family-owned Dolle's Candy on the boardwalk. She gave me a glimpse into maintaining and growing a family-owned business. Anna granted permission to use her family's historic photos.

Tommy Vann – Tommy and the Echoes performed at the Ship's Café and other Ocean City venues. I am fortunate to call him friend and to continue to see him perform in Baltimore County venues.

Mary David Rutka – I met Mary when we stayed at the Lankford Hotel with our grandchildren. She shared how committed she is to maintaining the historic character of her family's business.

Gus Lambros – Gus was a tough-minded businessman who operated and then owned the Lambros-Hampton House. Our family spent many happy summer weeks with him. Mr. Lambros, like many Ocean City historic hotel owners, would stay from May through September in Ocean City to make sure his guests were comfortable. Gus died in Towson, Maryland, on November 4, 2016.

Priscilla Grasmick-Stoney – Priscilla is my cousin. Her mom, Marie Swintech Knop, used to spend a month at the Majestic Hotel, often at the same time we were in Ocean City with our children and my mom, Dolores Knop Sprissler. Priscilla told me about why her Baltimore mother loved the Ocean.

Dona Ang Yates – Dona, an artist and teacher, and I spent hours recalling her Ocean City life and her connection to St. Mary's parish. Her great sense of humor is evident in the quotes I included.

Betsy Ludlam – Betsy is a longtime active parishioner of St. Mary Star of the Sea and Holy Savior. Her stories about Monsignor Stout and his dogs kept me laughing.

Mary Lou Jones – Mrs. Jones of St. Mary Star of the Sea recalls how many generations of parishioners returned to the parish for important occasions. Mary Lou personified the attachment of residents to their historic churches.

Nancy Sacca – Nancy's family home, the Esposito/Ludlam House in downtown Ocean City, was an historic landmark. She chaired the annual Holy Savior Christmas bazaar for 16 years. We chatted by phone before her death in 2013.

Marion Cropper – Marion is a longtime parishioner of St. Paul's By-the-Sea whom I interviewed by phone. Mrs. Cropper married into one of the two Cropper families. She laughed telling me, "...not the more famous Croppers."

Bob Stevens and Sandy Stevens – the Stevens are involved and longtime parishioners of St. Paul's By-the-Sea. They shared with me intimate details about the Church's fundraiser, "Antiques-By-the-Sea," and the church's outreach center, Red Door.

Charlotte Parker – Charlotte told me about her sewing and craft work sold at Antiques-By-the-Sea for the church's outreach work. She owned and operated the Beacon Apartments. Charlotte died in 2018.

June Todd – June is an active member of Atlantic Methodist Church. She told me about the parish's outreach work. Mrs. Todd was the author of the 90th anniversary book for Atlantic Methodist.

Jack Moore – Jack is a Baltimore transplant who moved to Ocean City and became active in Atlantic Methodist. Both June and Jack brought files for my research, which included historical information and clippings.

John Lynch – John manages and owns the Commander Hotel. The Lynch family built the hotel in 1930 at 14th and the Boardwalk. After my interview during our stay, John allowed me to take pictures of the lobby.

Donn Devine – Donn, a lawyer and writer, was the former archivist for the Diocese of Wilmington, DE, who pointed me to great resources on the Catholic Church's history in Ocean City. Donn died on May 5, 2019.

Thanks to the following who gave me permission to use photos in this publication:

- Father David Dingwall
- Anna Bushnell Dolle
- John Lynch
- Eugene Marshall
- Catherine Monius Merkel
- Dolores Monet
- David Sites
- The Ocean City Life-Saving Station Museum
- Tommy Vann Productions

Endnotes

1. A midden is defined as a mound of oyster shells. Archeologists found middens on the Ocean City beach dating back to when Native Americans fished the waters.

2. Michael Morgan, *Ocean City Going Down the Ocean*, (Charleston: The History Press, 2011), 11.

3. https://msa.maryland.gov//msa/mdmanual/01glance.native/html/01native.html#nanticoke

4. https://www.oceancitymd/oc-history

5. "Abandoned Rails", photo and commentary by Alan Snyder, September 23, 2009.

6. Sheri Reno. "Railway Brings Travelers," from The Tides and Times of Ocean City, The Ocean City Life-Saving Station Museum, 2014.

7. https://www.oceancitymd/oc-history

The Destination Beach

8. 2010 US Census records 7,102 permanent residents of Ocean City.https://www.census.gov

9. George and Susan Hurley, *A Pictorial History of Ocean City Maryland*, 12.

10. George Hurley was a teacher, a developer, a councilman and a life-long resident of Ocean City. He was an amateur historian and, with Susan his wife, founded the Ocean City Life-Saving Station Museum. I have drawn upon George's wit and wisdom many times in writing this book.

11. George Hurley, "Memories of Ocean City: 1950," Ocean City Life-Saving Station Museum website: https:// www.ocmuseum.org. 2007.

12. George and Susan Hurley, 12.

13. https://www.oceancitymd.com

14. Dolores Monet. *Ocean City Maryland – A Brief History of OCMD With Pictures.* Camping with the Kids comment on Monet's website. https://hubpages.com/@doloresmonet

15. Burt Raugley. "Summertime Jobs at Ocean City" on the Ocean City Lifesaving Museum website, https: www.ocmuseum.org. 2008.

16. Morgan, 55-56.

17. Mary L Martin and Nathaniel Wolfgang-Price, *Greetings from Ocean City.* (Atglen, Pennsylvania: Schifter Publishing, LTD 2009), 71.

18. Eben Davis, and Damon Talbot, "Summer Vacations: Greetings from Ocean City," The Underbelly, Maryland Historical Society, June 27, 2013.

19. Climate and Average Weather Year Round in Ocean City. https://www. weatherspark.com

20. John Hayden, "And Maryland on My Mind, An Ocean City Blog." https://marylandonmymind.wordpress.com.

21. Gerald W Johnson,. "A Road to Ocean City." *Baltimore Evening Sun*. February 15, 1940.

22. Bill Gibbs owned the Breakers Hotel, Dough Roller Restaurants, and Edward's on the boardwalk. He also invested in other properties in Ocean City. During my interview with Bill, he shared several stories of growing up at the resort and his earlier jobs. Bill and his brother had to give up their bedrooms in their parent's house on Baltimore Avenue to accommodate short-term renters. Bill said they slept on the porch during those nights.

23. Morgan, 96.

24. Joe Kro-Art is one of the most engaging business owners in Ocean City. He sees that "art is fun" and every inch of his gallery demonstrates that belief. Joe loves to talk about the works, his philosophy of engagement with the world, and the worldwide publicity Ocean Gallery enjoys.

25. www.oceangallery.com

26. https://singulart.com

27. Noted on the National Carousel Association's website. https://carousels.org

28. Monet. "Ocean City Maryland – A Brief History of OCMD with Pictures," 2.

29. Jake Fewster, "2012 Halloween Guide." *The Baltimore Sun*, October 12, 2012.

30. John Barth, *Lost in the Funhouse*. New York: Knopf Doubleday Publishing Group, 1988.

31. Monet. 10.

32. Andrea Bowland. Lord of the Fries: The Man Who Keeps a Watchful Eye Over Ocean City's Favorite Fries. Posted on "Shorebread" August 7, 2012.

33. Bowland.

34. Bowland.

35. Lynn Bartlet, Maryland on My Mind: An Ocean City Blog," https://marylandonmymind.wordpress.com .

36. History of Dolle's on their website www.dollestaffy.com .

37. Anna Bushnell Dolle manages the Dolle's on the boardwalk at Ocean City. She gave me an interview in between waiting on customers. Anna typifies the hard work and dedication of so many Ocean City business owners. They actually wait on customers and delight in the pleasure their businesses give to vacationers.

38. Dolle interview by Ellen Marshall..

39. www.wockenfusscandies.com.

40. www.thedoughroller.com.

41. Nancy Sacca's family were long time Ocean City residents. Their home was an historic landmark.

42. Martin and Wolfgang-Price, 84.

43. McDermott.

44. George and Susan Hurley, *Ocean City Maryland: A Pictorial History*. (Virginia: The Donning Company, 2011), 137.

45. Dona And Yates is an artist, teacher and great story teller. During our long interview over two afternoons, Dona told me so many interesting stories of her life in Ocean City.

46. Renee Antes. "A group of influential figures has helped define today's OC." https://www.DelmarvaNow, 2003

Where We Stay

47. https/www. oceancity.md estimates that the summer visitor population is within this range. A 2017 Comprehensive Plan stated that it is difficult to get an accurate reading of resort populations due to private rentals. Since the resort has conferences and special events all year, this site estimates an annual visitor count of 8 million.

48. https:/www.oceancity.com .The resort's tourism website states that there are 10,000 hotel units and more than 25,000 condominium units.

49. George and Susan Hurley,12.

50. Gordon E. Katz, *102 Gentlemen & a Lady: The Story of the Atlantic Hotel Company in Ocean City, Maryland*. (Missouri: Walsworth Publishing Company, 2012), p.76.

51. Bill Purnell described the history of his family's investment in Ocean City in an interview that took place in Layton's Restaurant after breakfast. In his own uncensored style, Mr. Purnell represents what I saw in many of my interviewees. The business community works hard to maintain the family-friendly atmosphere of the resort.

52. Katz, 83.

53. Bill Purnell interview by Ellen Marshall.

54. Purnell interview.

55. This is a message on the back of an Atlantic Hotel postcard.

56. Purnell interview.

57. Purnell interview.

58. Katz, 204.

59. Martin and Wolfgang-Price, 29.

60. Brian Shane. "Hotel Impossible to bring new reality to Maryland's ocean front." https://www.usatoday.com June 12, 2013.

61. OC Life and Times, OC Life-Saving Station Museum, "Looking Back to 1956," https: www/ocmuseum.org, 2006.

62. Gordon Katz, "Ocean City Then & Now – The Shoreham" OC Life and Times OC Life-Saving Station Museum. January 2019.

63. "The Haunted Trifecta #2. Ocean City Archives - Chesapeake Ghost Tours,"https://www.chesapeakeghosts.com

64. Over several stays at the Lankford, I was able to interview Mary four times. She is engaging and generous in sharing the challenges of operating an older facility. There is the annual costs of maintaining buildings which face the Ocean. Plus, it is difficult to invest in modern internet-based reservation systems, wi-fi, and other amenities offered by the newer hotels. However, the fact that they are staying in business after receiving a purchase offer shows how dedicated the family is to making sure the right company takes over.

65. Shane.

66. Shane.

67. Interview with Mary David Rutka by Ellen Marshall.

68. Priscilla Grasmick-Stoney interview by Ellen Marshall.

69. John Lynch gave rich details of the Commander's history and connection to other prominent Ocean City families.

70. Thomas D Winbrow. "The Commander Hotel: Maryland' Smartest Hotel -Assistant to the StoreKeeper," The Tides and Times of Ocean City, https: www/ocmuseum.org, 2006.

71. Mr. Gus Lambros was a great source of information about the struggles of maintaining a family-friendly older hotel with maintenance and staff challenges. He also discussed the push to change construction restrictions. As Gus saw it, if the Council would allow him to build up, he could hold onto the property and make it more profitable. Ironically, developers were able to add stories after the Lambros family sold. Mr. Lambros died in 2016.

72. Katz, 34.

73. Mary Adeline Bradford, , Editor. A Century of Celebration: St. Paul's By-The-Sea Episcopal Church Ocean City Maryland, Texas: Taylor Publishing Company, 1999, p.24.

74. Charlotte Cropper Interview by Ellen Marshall.

75. "The Petticoat Regime of 1890 to 1926." The Tide and Times of Ocean City. https: www.ocmuseum.org. 2006.

76. Martin and Wolfgang-Price,32.

77. Dona Ang Yates interview by Ellen Marshall.

78. https: harrisonhalloc.com.

79. Martin and Wolfgang-Price, 28.

80. Interview with Bill Gibbs by Ellen Marshall.

81. Interview with George Hurley by Ellen Marshall.

Where We Eat

82. www.visitmd.org

83. Staff Writer, "40 Years and Counting For Layton's Dip n' Donuts In OC." *Ocean City Dispatch*, May 23, 2008.

84. Staff Writer.

85. Pam Layton is always busy at her family restaurant. She waits tables, checks out customers, and, in my case, fits in an interview between tables.

86. Pam Layton interview by Ellen Marshall.

87. Pam Layton interview.

88. Pam Layton interview.

89. www.thrashersfries.com

90. Marisa Pouison, "Fishing Seasons in Ocean City, Maryland," *USA Today* Travel Tips, March 15, 2018.

91. Matthew Wight. "Lessons Learned; the Never-ending Search for a Purposeful & Significant Life", 2008.

92. www.angleroc.net

93. Maddie Aiken. "Phillips Seafood, an Ocean City icon, closes doors permanently." *Salisbury Daily Times*, Published December 20, 2021). https://www. DelmarvaNow.com

94. Drew Lazor and Lizzie Munro. "The Rise of Baltimore's Orange Crush Cocktail," https://www.ClubPlanet.com

95. www.embers.com

Where We Worship

96. Ocean City land records. https://www.co.worcester.md.us.

97. Gordon E. Katz, "Ocean City Maryland: Saint Mary Star Of The Sea Catholic Church 'An Ocean City Original, '"http://www.ocmuseum.org/index.php/site/oc-history_article/saint_mary_star_of_the_sea, 2.

98. Author Unknown. "History of the Catholic Church of Ocean City Maryland" circa 1954, 3.

99. Geoffry H. Robbins DDS and Brian P Henley, History of Ocean City 1875-1975. Reprinted in *Eastern Shore Times* and *Maryland Beachcomber*, 1975, 56.

100. Author Unknown, 2.

101. Jeane C Kolaris, "The Cutting Edge: The Life of Thomas A. Becker". Chapter 5, "Funding A Diocese." This is an excerpt from ADW, Becker Daybook, p. 13, April 19, 1872. APF ser.rif.A.C. vol. 26, folio 332v,333 r. Note Z: the letter is in Italian.

102. Kolaris, p.100. Becker is speaking about the need for the order to stay on the Shore, even though the counties are poor and "never supported a pastor."

103. "Baltimore Catechism One," The Third Plenary Council of Baltimore, first published in 1885. I am quoting from memory going back to my parochial school days.

104. Michael Morgan, "Ocean City: Going Down the Ocean," (Charleston, the History Press, 2011), 47.

105. Author unknown, "History....Original", p.2.

106. Author unknown, "History....Original", p.2.

107. L.A.R. "A Few Words About The Parish," in Blessing of the New Pipe Organ St. Mary's Star of The Sea. Ocean City, Maryland: August 24, 1941.

108. http://www.ocmuseum.org/index.php/site/oc-history_article/saint_mary_star_of_the_sea , p.2.

109. Dona Ang Yates interview by Ellen Marshall.

110. Robbins, Geoffry H.,DDS and Henley, Brian P. History of Ocean City 1875-1975. Reprinted in *Eastern Shore Times* and *Maryland Beachcomber*, 1975, p.57.

111. Robbins and Henley, p. 54.

112. Yates interview.

113. Author unknown. "History of the Catholic Church of Ocean City, Maryland," circa 1954, p. 10.

114. Author unknown, p. 10.

115. Dolores Monet.

116. Yates interview.

117. Mary Lou Jones interview. Mary Lou has been a parishioner of St. Mary's since 1968 and a member of the parish council.

118. Jones interview by Ellen Marshall.

119. By the 1950s, St. Mary's and Holy Savior offered 9 masses on summer weekends. Source: Author unknown. "History of the Catholic Church of Ocean City, Maryland," circa 1954, p. 10.

120. Betsy Ludlam interview by Ellen Marshall. Betsy has been an active member of St. Mary's since 1951.

121. Jones interview.

122. Ludlam interview.

123. Jones interview.

124. Jones interview.

125. Ludlam interview.

126. The Episcopal Church is the American arm of the Anglican Church which was established during Henry VIII's reign. The Anglican Church broke away from Roman Catholicism in response to Henry's desire to divorce Anne Boleyn.

127. Gordon E.Katz, "St. Paul's By-The-Sea Episcopal Church: An Episcopal Ministry in Ocean City Maryland. http://www.ocmuseum.org/index.php/site/oc-history_article/st_pauls-by-the-sea-episcopal, 2010, 1.

128. Mary Adeline Bradford, ed,. A Century of Celebration: St. Paul's By-The-Sea Episcopal Church, Ocean City, Maryland. Dallas, Texas: Taylor Publishing Company, 1999, 6-7.

129. Katz,1.

130. Bradford, 9.

131. "Timeline of St. Paul's by-the-Sea Church and Early Worcester Parishes," an unpublished archival document.

132. Katz, 3.

133. Katz, 3.

134. Author unknown. "St. Paul's By-The-Sea Episcopal Church: An Episcopal Ministry in Ocean City, Maryland." Un-numbered, 6.

135. Above, 6.

136. John Parisi, An unpublished body of research on the life of Bishop Curtis. Researcher is a volunteer in the Wilmington Diocese Archive Department.

137. Katz, 5.

138. Katz, 5.

139. Katz, 7.

140. Excerpt from a telephone interview with Mrs. Cropper by Ellen Marshall.

141. Bradford, 53.

142. Bradford, 30.

143. June Todd, "Celebrating 90 Years of Ministry in Ocean City, Maryland, 1915-2005," October 23, 2005, 1.

144. Todd, 1.

145. Interview with June Todd and Jack Moore by Ellen Marshall.

146. Interview with Todd and Moore.

147. Morgan, 29.

148. Nan DeVincent-Hayes, Ph.D. and John E Jacob. *Images of America Ocean City, Volume II.* Charleston: Arcadia Publishing, 1999. 96.

149. DeVincent-Hayes and Jacob, 93.

150. Website http://templebatyam-oc.org, About Us/TBY Community page.

151. George and Susan Hurley. *A Pictorial History of Ocean City Maryland*. 12.

Characters

152. John Lewis, "Boardwalk Empire: Joe Kro-Art created an Ocean City landmark out of old junk, new art, and timeless showmanship," *Baltimore Magazine,* August 2013.

153. Lewis.

154. Bucky Mann. "Vanishing Ocean City." Posted on 7/03/2014 on the website, https://mdcoastdispatch.com.

155. For years the early history of the carousel maintained it was purchased in 1902, rather than the actual date of 1912. It wasn't until Gordon Katz was researching his book on the Atlantic Hotel that the 1912 date surfaced.

156. Bucky Mann, "Vanishing Ocean City" *Maryland Coast Dispatch*. July 24, 2014. https://mdcoastdispatch.com .

157. Morgan, 62-63.

158. Dale Timmons, "OC's Fishing Heritage" https://www.fishinoc.com.

159. Shawn Soper, "OC's Fish Powell Remembered Fondly as a Mentor, Friend, Leader. OC Today . August 30, 2018.

160. Editorial "Bobby Baker and the rise of good times in Ocean City." *OC Today*, November 22, 2017.

161. Jon Thurber, 'Bobby Baker, protégé of Lyndon Johnson felled by influence-peddling scandal dies at 89." *The Washington Post*, November 17, 2017.

162. "Major Political Scandal Looming in the Bobby Baker Case; Ax It Becomes Further Unraveled Many Persons Are Expected to Be Named as Having a Role in His Wheelings and Dealings." *The New York Times*, January 26, 1964.

163. Kara Hallissey, "Ocean City icon, 'Boardwalk Elvis,' honored at event. *OC Today*, 12/12/2014.

164. Posted on December 15, 2014 by atomictv.

165. Dail Willis, "Walking the Boards with Elvis of O.C." The Ocean City bureau of *The Sun*.

166. Local East Baltimore dialect for "down the ocean."

Ellen's Favorite Places

Ocean Gallery World Center
https://www.facebook.com/oceangalleryworldcenter/
201 N. Boardwalk
(410) 289-5300

Ocean City Life Saving Museum
https://ocmuseum.org
813 S. Atlantic Avenue
(410) 289-4991

Paradise Plaza
https://paradiseplazainn.com
3 9th Street
(888) 678-4111

The Lankford
www.lankfordhotel.com
807 N. Atlantic Avenue
(800) 282-9709

The Majestic Hotel
https://ocmajestichotel.com
613 N. Boardwalk
(410) 289-6262

The Commander Hotel
www.commanderhotel.com
1405 Baltimore Avenue
(888) 289-6166

Tidelands Caribbean Hotel
www.tidelandscaribbean.com
409 Atlantic Avenue
(410) 289-9455

Coins Pub & Restaurant
www.coinspuboc.com
2820 Philadelphia Avenue
(410) 289-3100

9th Street Taphouse
www.octaphouses.com
9th Street and Boardwalk
(443) 664-2641

4th Street Taphouse
www.octaphouses.com
407 Atlantic Avenue
(410) 390-3685

45th Street Taphouse
www.octaphouses.com
4507 Coastal Highway
(443) 664-2201

Taphouse Tavern
www.octaphouses.com
13729 Coastal Highway
(410) 390-7845

Layton's
https://laytons1601.wixsite.com/laytons16restaurant
1601 Philadelphia Avenue
(410) 289-6635

Harborside Bar & Grill
https://weocharborside.com
12841 S. Harbor Road
(410) 213-1846

The Crab Stop
www.crabstopoc.com
1511 Philadelphia Avenue
(410) 289-3020

Thrasher's French Fries
www.thrashersfries.com
401 Atlantic Avenue #1
(410) 289-7232

Candy Kitchen
www.candykitchen.com
203 North Boardwalk
(410) 289-2121

Dolle's Candyland
www.dolles.com
500 S. Atlantic Avenue, Suite 1
(410) 289-6000

Wockenfuss Candy
www.wockenfusscandies.com
Boardwalk and 1st Street
(410) 289-5054

Soriano's Coffee Shop and Restaurant
www.sorianoscoffeeshop.com
306 S. Baltimore Avenue
(410) 289-6656

Bayside Skillet
https://thebaysideskillet.com
7701 Coastal Highway
(410) 524-7950

Sanibal Jewelry
401 S. Atlantic Avenue
(410) 289-5002

Sea Trader Gift Shop
807 Atlantic (underneath the boards at The Lankford Hotel)
(410) 289-8232

CPSIA information can be obtained
at www.ICGtesting.com
Printed in the USA
BVHW020338020522
635809BV00018BA/516